A 90-DAY DEVOTIONAL

# A
# MAN
## OF
# PURPOSE
## AND
# POWER

## DR. MYLES MUNROE

WHITAKER
HOUSE

## A MAN OF PURPOSE AND POWER:
### *A 90-Day Devotional*

Munroe Global
P.O. Box N9583
Nassau, Bahamas
www.munroeglobal.com
office@munroeglobal.com

ISBN: 978-1-64123-654-6 • eBook ISBN: 978-1-64123-655-3
Printed in the United States of America
© 2021 by Munroe Group of Companies Ltd.

Whitaker House
1030 Hunt Valley Circle
New Kensington, PA 15068
www.whitakerhouse.com

Library of Congress Control Number: 2021937153

2  3  4  5  6  7  8  9  10  11  **W**  28  27  26  25  24  23  22

# CONTENTS

# INTRODUCTION

For thirty years, Dr. Myles Munroe studied, counseled, and guided thousands of individuals to live lives of personal fulfillment and social and spiritual well-being. The knowledge and experience he gained led him to the conclusion that the central principle of life is *purpose*. Yet, as he described in his book *Understanding the Purpose and Power of Men*, today, "many men are questioning who they are and what roles they are to play in life. On the surface, they may be following customary life pursuits, such as working, marrying, and having a family. Yet they have an inner uncertainty about what it means to be a man, a husband, and a father.

"What is causing this uncertainty? A major reason is that society is sending out conflicting signals about what it means to be a man. Traditional views of masculinity compete side by side with new ideas of manhood in the marketplace of ideas—each vying for supremacy....

"Historically, men have defined their manhood by the various roles they have fulfilled for their families and for society. Now that these roles are in transition, they don't have a solid definition of masculinity to give them a cultural context for life. As a result, many men believe they have lost part of themselves, but they don't have anything concrete with which to replace it. Often, they don't even feel wanted or needed by women any longer. They used to have clear direction about where they were going as men. Now, it's as if they're trapped in a maze, frustrated and unable to move forward purposefully in life....

"People can go for years without realizing they aren't fulfilling their true purpose. Both individuals and cultures can become comfortable following established roles without questioning their validity. However, our socially turbulent society is forcing us to examine the underlying foundation of our concepts of maleness and femaleness. In this sense, we can look at this crisis as a powerful opportunity for self-discovery and self-actualization. It is up to us to make accurate tests of the soundness of both traditional and contemporary ideas of what it means to be male and female, and then to relay a strong foundation for society."

Dr. Munroe came to the conclusion that "male identity is not essentially a matter of *roles*, which vary with culture and shift with changing times—it is a matter of *inherent purpose*." He wrote, "How do we measure a man? What is true manhood? How do you define masculinity? What is true male sexuality? What is the true purpose of the male in relation to the female? Is there a universal definition of manhood? Can it be attained? Where do we go to get this definition?

"This book addresses answers to these critical questions from the perspective of the male. The purpose and role of the male in the scheme of human experience is explored through returning to the original process of his creation, based on the premise that no one knows the product like the manufacturer. No product can understand its identity by asking the customer, because only the manufacturer knows the original purpose and potential of his product. Therefore, it is imperative that the male rediscover his original purpose and understand his true potential, as well as gain a clear understanding of his principal function within the human family.

"The male is the key to building strong, enduring social infrastructures, stable families, sane societies, and secure nations. It is critical that the subject of the male's crisis be a priority for men, women, and national governments, so that we can secure progressive social developments within the countries of the world. Let us begin our journey through the land of cultural confusion to rediscover the purpose and power of the real male."

From his study of the Scriptures, Dr. Munroe believed that men have a unique purpose in God's plan for the world. As you progress through these ninety devotionals, you will discover biblical truths and principles that explain men's distinct and complementary design to women and find practical application for implementing what you learn into your daily life.

Also featured are daily Scripture readings, with one Old Testament passage and one New Testament passage for each day. Since we find our purpose only in the mind of our Maker, it is essential to read His "Manual," as Dr. Munroe liked to call the Bible, for ourselves in order to clearly see the revelation of His purposes. We must allow God's Word to dwell richly in our hearts so that, as we meditate on and absorb Scripture, it truly becomes a part of our lives.

Whenever we study the Word of God, we should also pray and ask God for wisdom. The Holy Spirit is our Teacher, and we need to ask Him to illuminate the Word and give us insight.

You can discover how to live according to God's plan, so you can become all you were created to be as a unique man made in His image—*A Man of Purpose and Power*. May God bless you in your relationship with Him and with those He has placed in your life as you fulfill that distinct purpose.

# —Day 1—
## DO YOU KNOW WHERE
## YOU'RE HEADED?

*"In their hearts humans plan their course, but the LORD establishes their steps."* —Proverbs 16:9

I was driving along an undeveloped street near my home one day when I saw a large sign with a beautifully painted picture of a building. The sign said, COMING SOON. I sensed the Holy Spirit saying to me, "Did you see that?" I asked, "See what?" He said, "Did you see the finish?" I came back around to take another look at the painting, and the Holy Spirit continued, "If you were to see the men working on that project, digging up all the mud and muck, making big holes, and if you were to ask them what they were doing, they would say, 'We are building that.' They could tell you exactly where they were headed." I have never forgotten that lesson.

I have some questions for you: Is your life similar to that? If someone were to ask you where you're going, could you answer that you're headed somewhere? Could you specify where? Are you so clear about your dream that you could paint a picture of it?

If you know where you're going, then when someone doesn't understand the reason for "the mud, the muck, the water, and the hole," it doesn't matter. Everything might look in disarray, but you know it is part of the process. And when you're in the midst of the process, your life might not seem like it's becoming anything. But take careful note: there's a painting of you. God has painted it for you in His Word. Anytime you get bogged down, every time you get discouraged, you can look at that painting.

We may be able to see the outcome of God's purposes for our lives twenty years into the future—or only one day ahead. Yet if we are living in God's plans for us, we have found the key to our existence.

Dear Father, You are the Creator, the Maker of all things—including me. You have a purpose for my creation beyond anything I can easily understand. Help me to keep my eyes upon You and Your Word as You reveal my purpose on this earth. In Jesus's name, amen.

*Thought:* If someone were to ask you where you're going in life, what would you answer?

*Readings:* Proverbs 16:1–20; Ephesians 5:15–20

# —Day 2—
## STOPPED IN THE MIDDLE OF TRAFFIC

*"For as the heavens are higher than the earth, so are My ways higher than your ways, and My thoughts than your thoughts."*     —Isaiah 55:9 (NKJV)

It is dangerous to live without God! If you don't know God, you'll never know your reason for existence. And if you don't know why you were born, you could live a completely wrong life.

One of the reasons Jesus knew His purpose was that He was continually seeking God and in constant communication with Him. That is the pattern each of us needs to follow. Why? There are many good people who are pursuing relationships, careers, and goals in life that are not best for them. What we have to concern ourselves with is living effectively. The only way to live a fulfilled life is to know why you were born. The only way to know why you were born is to learn it from the One who created you.

Have you ever had a new car break down on you right in the middle of traffic? You got out and kicked one of the tires. Maybe you just wanted to curse at it because the car wasn't fulfilling its purpose. It was brand-new. It looked sleek. It had a nice paint job. But you couldn't drive it. What made you angry at the car? It's simple: the car's purpose was to transport you, to make you mobile; but the car was not taking you anywhere. No matter how great the car looked, it wasn't right; it wasn't fulfilling its purpose.

Many men are like that car. They're stopped in the middle of traffic, and they don't even realize it. They're spending their lives doing things that look good, but they don't know God—or they know too little about Him and His ways.

God has special plans for you, if you will be who He created you to be. He has given you your personality and gifts for a specific reason. *"For we are God's workmanship, created in Christ Jesus to do good works, which God prepared in advance for us to do"* (Ephesians 2:10 NIV84).

*Thought:* Knowing and fulfilling your purpose is the only way to do what is right.

*Readings:* Isaiah 55:6–9; Ephesians 2:1–10

# —DAY 3—
## UNDERSTANDING YOUR PURPOSE

*"The law of the LORD is perfect, refreshing the soul. The statutes of the LORD are trustworthy, making wise the simple."*
—Psalm 19:7

The great challenge of life is understanding life. When life throws us a curveball, we often just play games and fake it. Many times, we have to guess and then wonder endlessly if our guesses will work.

What we lack is understanding. David, the great king of Israel, made an observation regarding this very issue. By divine inspiration, he spoke of the moral and social chaos in his community and described the root cause of humanity's confusion, frustration, and self-destruction: "[They] *know nothing, they understand nothing. They walk about in darkness; all the foundations of the earth are shaken*" (Psalm 82:5).

This text declares that the reason why the people of the earth are so confused and filled with problems is not because there are no answers but because we don't understand our Creator. We don't know His principles, His purpose, His nature, or His precepts.

The greatest enemy of mankind is *ignorance of self*. Nothing is more frustrating than not knowing who you are or what to do with what you have. All of humanity's problems are a result of this major dilemma. Essentially, the dilemma is that we lack understanding. Without understanding, life is an experiment, and frustration is the reward.

But learning God's ways will transform your spirit, your mind, and your outlook. When you present yourself to God and learn from Him, you will begin to understand His purpose. *"The law of* the LORD is perfect, refreshing the soul. *The statutes of the LORD are trustworthy, making wise the simple"* (Psalm 19:7).

The greatest way for you to find purpose is to yield your life to the Manufacturer. You shouldn't come to God because it's the religious thing to do. You shouldn't come to God because "everybody" is doing it. You shouldn't come to God because it's good to be a part of the church. You should come to God because you want to find out how not to waste your life. No one knows you like the One who made you. That's the bottom line.

We are so special to God that He sent His only Son to die for us. There must be something unique about each one of us for God to want us to receive salvation so that we can fulfill the purpose for which He gave us life. We need to seek Him earnestly in order to discover that purpose. *"You will seek me and find me when you seek me with all your heart"* (Jeremiah 29:13).

~

*Thought:* The greatest way for you to find purpose is to yield your life to the Manufacturer.

*Readings:* Psalm 19; Matthew 11:25–28

# — DAY 4 —
## SEVEN PRINCIPLES OF PURPOSE

"[God] *works out everything in conformity with the purpose of his will.*"                                    —Ephesians 1:11

The source of so many of our problems in this world is that we have lost our understanding of what it means to be human as God created us. We have lost our sense of purpose. I am convinced that, in every country in the world, both men and women are suffering from this ignorance of purpose. The best thing for us to do is to discover and live in the original plan of the One who created humanity. Only then will we learn the inherent nature and rights of men and women, so that both male and female can live in freedom and fulfillment.

The following seven principles of purpose will help us to understand God's original intent for us in creation:

1. God is a God of purpose.

2. God created everything with a purpose.

3. Not every purpose is known to us because we have lost our understanding of God's original intent for us.

4. Where purpose is not known, abuse is inevitable.

5. To discover the purpose of something, never ask the creation; ask the creator.

6. We find our purpose only in the mind of our Maker.

7. God's purpose is the key to our fulfillment.

God is a purposeful Being. He purposes, He plans, and then He carries out His plans. God always knew what He wanted to create before He made it; similarly, He always knows what He wants to carry out before He accomplishes it.

This theme is found throughout the Bible, which we can consider God's handbook, or manual, for our lives. Here are various expressions of His purposeful nature:

> And God said, "Let there be light," and there was light.
> (Genesis 1:3)

> The plans of the LORD stand firm forever, the purposes of his heart through all generations. (Psalm 33:11)

> The LORD Almighty has sworn, "Surely, as I have planned, so it will be, and as I have purposed, so it will happen." (Isaiah 14:24)

> As the rain and the snow come down from heaven, and do not return to it without watering the earth and making it bud and flourish, so that it yields seed for the sower and bread for the eater, so is my word that goes out from my mouth: It will not return to me empty, but will accomplish what I desire and achieve the purpose for which I sent it. (Isaiah 55:10–11)

> God…has saved us and called us to a holy life—not because of anything we have done but because of his own purpose and grace. This grace was given us in Christ Jesus before the beginning of time. (2 Timothy 1:8–9)

We have been created purposefully by God. Only when we fully understand this concept will we see how important it is for our well-being that we discover God's intent for us.

⌒

*Thought*: God is a God of purpose.

*Readings*: Meditate on the above passages from the Old and New Testaments.

# —Day 5—
## GOD WILL FULFILL HIS PURPOSES

*"The plans of the Lord stand firm forever, the purposes of his heart through all generations."*          —Psalm 33:11

God is purposeful, and He always carries out His purposes. Let's review some Scripture verses from Isaiah and Hebrews that illustrate a vital aspect of God's purposeful nature.

*The Lord Almighty has sworn, "Surely, as I have planned, so it will be, and as I have purposed, so it will happen."*
(Isaiah 14:24)

The first part of this verse states that God has sworn an oath. Now, when people swear an oath, they have to find something higher than themselves by which to swear. As we read in Hebrews 6:16, *"People swear by someone greater than themselves, and the oath confirms what is said and puts an end to all argument."* We usually swear by the Bible or by some great institution. But when God swears an oath, there is no one above Him. So, He has to swear by Himself.

If you were called to be a witness in court, you would be asked to swear on the Bible, "I swear to tell the truth, the whole truth, and nothing but the truth, so help me, God." If you were to lie, it would be the same as desecrating the integrity of the Bible, and you would destroy your own integrity as well.

When God swears an oath regarding something, He fulfills what He has sworn to do because He is totally faithful to Himself. God doesn't want us to have any doubt about this aspect of His nature.

*Because God wanted to make the unchanging nature of his purpose very clear to the heirs of what was promised, he confirmed it with an oath.* (Hebrews 6:17)

We can be assured that God will fulfill His purposes for us as we allow Christ the Redeemer to restore us to Him and to the purposes He has for us.

⌒

*Thought:* God is purposeful, and He always carries out His purposes.

*Readings:* Psalm 33; Hebrews 6:13–20

# GOD CREATED EVERYTHING
# WITH A PURPOSE

*"Star differs from star in splendor ["glory" NKJV]."*
—1 Corinthians 15:41

Purpose is the original intent of a creator in the creation of something. It is what is in the creator's mind that causes him to fashion his product in a certain manner. In short, purpose motivates the action of creation. This results in precision production.

Everything that God has made in this life has a purpose. One of the essential principles of purpose is that "the purpose of something determines its nature or design." We can fight against God's purposes for us, but if we do, we will be unfulfilled and frustrated. He made us the way we are for His purposes and for our benefit.

Since God is a God of purpose, He never created anything hoping that it would turn out to be something viable. He first decided what it was to be, then He made it. He always begins with a finished product in mind.

Consider these questions:

+ Why are humans different from animals?
+ Why is a bird different from a fish?
+ Why is the sun different from the moon?
+ Why does one star differ from another star?
+ Why are men different from women?

I will answer these questions with this statement: Everything is the way it is because of why it was created, because of its purpose. The *why* dictates the design. God created everything with the ability to fulfill its purpose. Therefore, to understand how we function as human beings, we have to go to the Manual given to us by the Designer and Manufacturer who created us.

"*People have one kind of flesh, animals have another, birds another and fish another*" (1 Corinthians 15:39). Of course, the word "*flesh*" in this instance does not refer to meat; instead, it refers to the nature of the creature—its characteristic design. God determined that human beings would be different from animals in their nature. He also determined that birds and fish would have distinct natures. The passage goes on to say,

> *There are also heavenly bodies and there are earthly bodies; but the splendor* ["glory" NKJV] *of the heavenly bodies is one kind, and the splendor* ["glory" NKJV] *of the earthly bodies is another. The sun has one kind of splendor* ["glory" NKJV], *the moon another and the stars another; and star differs from star in splendor* ["glory" NKJV].     (1 Corinthians 15:40–41)

The sun is meant to do a job that the moon isn't supposed to do, so God created the moon different from the sun. The moon is made to do its job, and no other job. The moon does not give light; it reflects light. Therefore, God did not put any light on the moon. God also made stars of different sizes and luminosity, for His own purposes. The point is that God made everything the way it is because of what it is supposed to do. And that includes us!

⌣⌣

*Thought*: To understand how we function as human beings, we have to go to the Manual given to us by the Designer and Manufacturer who created us.

*Readings*: Genesis 1:1–26; Ephesians 1:3–14

# NOT EVERY PURPOSE IS KNOWN TO US

*"Your word is a lamp for my feet, a light on my path."*
—Psalm 119:105

Everything God created has a purpose and is designed according to that purpose. However, not every purpose is known to us. Humanity has lost its knowledge of God's purposes. It has not respected the fact that God's creation and His directions for living were established for a specific reason and that, if this purpose is abandoned, we will never function properly as human beings. The result of this abandonment has been debilitating for us: we have grown further and further away from God's original intent and design, so that we function less and less as we were meant to. This has left us incomplete, frustrated, and in conflict with one another.

The first chapter of Romans explains that when people reject or are ignorant of the purposes of God, they end up continually abusing themselves. They abuse their bodies, their minds, their relationships, and their talents.

*Although they knew God, they neither glorified him as God nor gave thanks to him, but their thinking became futile and their foolish hearts were darkened.*          (Romans 1:21)

This verse describes those who did not know the purpose of God and did not even care to find out what it is. Even though they knew something about God and His ways, they did not want Him in their lives. They did not want to know what He wanted them to know. They were saying, in effect, "Keep Your opinions about who we are to Yourself, God. We know You made us, but mind Your own business. We know You're there, but leave us alone."

The next verses tell us the result of their decision: *"Although they claimed to be wise, they became fools"* (Romans 1:22). They *"exchanged the truth about God for a lie"* and *"exchanged natural sexual relations for unnatural ones"* (verses 25–26).

When does the exchange of natural for unnatural take place? It takes place when purpose is either ignored or unknown. *"Furthermore, just as they did not think it worthwhile to retain the knowledge of God, so God gave them over to a depraved mind, so that they do what ought not to be done"* (verse 28). They didn't think it worthwhile to find out God's purpose for the world or to retain the knowledge of God as to why He made humanity. They didn't check to find out why God made men and women. They didn't try to find out what God knows about the things He has made. They didn't want to know, so they relied on their own inclinations.

The above statements from Romans are a description of humanity as a whole. We have rejected knowing God and His purposes, and so God's original intent for us has not been communicated in many of our cultures and traditions. It has been lost or obscured. Instead, distorted views have been passed down, so that people do not know how to relate to one another as they were meant to. This is the situation people often find themselves in. That is why it is essential for us to recover our original purpose in God.

*Thought*: We have grown further and further away from God's original intent and design, so that we function less and less as we were meant to.

*Readings*: Psalm 119:97–112; Romans 1:16–32

# WHERE PURPOSE IS UNKNOWN, ABUSE IS INEVITABLE

*"There is a way that appears to be right, but in the end it leads to death."*                                                   —Proverbs 14:12

You cannot move away from God and be truly successful. You cannot cut off your relationship with the Manufacturer and expect to find genuine parts somewhere else. When you ignore the warranty, any part you try to find on your own will not be genuine. You cannot develop into a better "product" without the help of the Manufacturer.

If we think we can find out how to be a better person without God, we are in trouble, for the consequences are serious. When we believe that we don't need God, we get worse and worse. How many people have been suffering from these very consequences?

*"Many are the plans in a person's heart, but it is the* LORD's *purpose that prevails"* (Proverbs 19:21). We have many plans, but God has a purpose. Our plans may not be in harmony with God's purpose. I think it is appropriate to include the concept of opinions or perceptions in the word *"plans."* We have many opinions and perceptions regarding what things should be like or what they are for, but God has a purpose for everything that He made. Therefore, what you think the purpose of something is, and what its purpose actually is, could be different.

The problem is that, if your plans are not in keeping with God's purpose, then you will either suffer yourself or inflict abuse on others, because where purpose is not known, abuse is inevitable. If you don't know the purpose of something, all you will do is abuse it, no matter how sincere, committed, serious, or innocent you are.

If you don't want to live in God's purpose for mankind, then you will end up doing yourself harm in some way. God has created us with gifts and talents that are intended to be used to fulfill His purposes. Yet since we often don't know how they are to be used, we take the talents He has given us and use them against ourselves and others.

Remember that God did not venture out into the manufacturing business hoping He could create something that would work. He started out with an original design in mind, and His finished product parallels His intended purpose. He is the only One who knows how humanity is intended to successfully function.

⸻

*Thought*: God has created us with gifts and talents that are intended to be used to fulfill His purposes.

*Readings*: Proverbs 14:6–9; Ephesians 5:1–14

# — DAY 9 —
## TO DISCOVER PURPOSE, NEVER ASK THE CREATION—ASK THE CREATOR

*"Yet you, LORD, are our Father. We are the clay, you are the potter; we are all the work of your hand."*     —Isaiah 64:8

We have seen that nobody knows a product and how it should work better than the one who made it. In the same way, the one who created the product is the best one to fix it when it has become marred. When a potter works on a pot and sees that it has a flaw in it, the potter either remolds the clay and starts over, or if the pot already has been fired in an oven, the potter has to smash it and start over.

Now, when the clay starts talking back to the potter, something is wrong. (See Isaiah 29:16.) The potter knows better than the pot how the pot should be fashioned. The pot can't say to the potter, "You shouldn't have made me this way," because the pot can't see the whole picture the way the potter can. When it comes to the relationship between males and females, we have too often murmured against the Potter rather than trying to understand how and why we were created. Moreover, our substitutes for His master design are flawed. Some of us need to have our attitudes, perspectives, and lives remolded. A few of us have gone so far in the wrong direction that we may need a total overhaul. God's principles are very serious and very awesome, but also very necessary for the restoration of humanity to God's purposes.

So if you want to discover the purpose of something, never ask the creation; ask the one who made it. The creation might not think it has any worth, but the creator knows what it is made of. Many people do not think they have any worth or purpose. Yet the first chapter of our Manual tells us, *"God saw all that he had made, and it was very good"* (Genesis 1:31). There is something good in God's creation, no matter how confused it looks to us. There is something good about every person, even though it may be hard to find. There is something good about everything God has made. We need to go to Him to find the good purposes for which He has made us. *"For it is God who works in you to will and to act in order to fulfill his good purpose"* (Philippians 2:13).

~~~~

*Thought*: The one who created the product is the best one to fix it when it has become marred.

*Readings*: Jeremiah 18:1–6; Philippians 2:12–16

# — Day 10 —
## WE FIND OUR PURPOSE ONLY IN OUR MAKER

*"As for God, his way is perfect: the* Lord's *word is flawless; he shields all who take refuge in him."* —Psalm 18:30

When we try to mend our relationships or change society using our own methods, we never totally succeed, and we often utterly fail. We fail because we are trying to bring about change for the wrong reasons and using the wrong methods. That is why we need to go back to the Manufacturer and receive His instructions for our lives. The only way for us to succeed is to discover and live in the purposes of our Maker by undergoing a transformation in the way we think about ourselves as human beings.

Romans 12:1–2 encourages us to give ourselves to God so that we may receive His principles for living rather than conforming to this world's pattern of living:

> *Offer your bodies as a living sacrifice, holy and pleasing to God—this is your true and proper worship. Do not conform to the pattern of this world, but be transformed by the renewing of your mind. Then you will be able to test and approve what God's will is—his good, pleasing and perfect will.*

In other words, we are not to conform to this world's opinions of humanity's purpose but be transformed into God's original intent in creation so that we can live in peace with ourselves and others. We do this by presenting our bodies to God, so they can line up with His purpose for our bodies, and by presenting our minds to Him, so they can line up with His purpose for our minds. Our minds are to be transformed as they are renewed.

Then we will truly be able to know *"what God's will is—his good, pleasing and perfect will."*

Many of us don't know God's perfect purpose for our bodies. We've been abusing them—selling them cheaply, filling them with alcohol, drugs, nicotine, or too much food. We've been making a mess of our lives.

Our bodies are meant to be God's temple. When you present your body to the Manufacturer, what does He do with it? He fills it with His own Spirit so you can be filled with His life and purpose. *"Do you not know that your bodies are temples of the Holy Spirit, who is in you, whom you have received from God? You are not your own"* (1 Corinthians 6:19).

When you present your spirit to the Manufacturer, it becomes *"the candle of the LORD"* (Proverbs 20:27 KJV), an expression of the light of God. It is the same way when you present your mind and soul to your Maker. They are renewed by His Word, which is a light for your path. (See Psalm 119:105.) David said, *"The law of the LORD is perfect, converting the soul; the testimony of the LORD is sure, making wise the simple"* (Psalm 19:7 NKJV). God's ways will transform your spirit, your mind, and your outlook. When you present yourself to God and learn from Him, you will understand His purpose.

Therefore, in order to pursue God's purpose, you first must present yourself to God, so that you can *know* His perfect will. Then you will be transformed, so that you can *do* His perfect will. In this way, His good purposes will be fulfilled in you.

⌒

*Thought*: We need to undergo a transformation in the way we think about ourselves as human beings.

*Readings*: Psalm 18:1–2, 30–36; Romans 12

# — Day 11 —
## GOD'S PURPOSE IS THE KEY TO OUR FULFILLMENT

*"Forgetting what is behind and straining toward what is ahead, I press on toward the goal to win the prize for which God has called me heavenward in Christ Jesus."*
—Philippians 3:13–14

Since everything God created was intentional, we can conclude that males and females were created intentionally. God didn't wonder why He made them or what their purpose should be after He created them. They were created to help fulfill God's eternal purpose. His eternal purpose is great, and within His larger purpose, He has many smaller purposes. Both the male and the female are to discover their individual purposes, which are part of God's larger plan.

The key thoughts we have been addressing in this devotional are that God has a purpose for everything and that He will always accomplish His purpose in the end. The best way to experience fulfillment in your life is to find God's purpose and then work with Him to fulfill it. Our Scripture reading for the previous entry included the following: *"Therefore, I urge you, brothers and sisters, in view of God's mercy, to offer your bodies as a living sacrifice, holy and pleasing to God—this is your true and proper worship"* (Romans 12:1). Becoming what God has purposed for us is an act of worship to our Creator.

In the devotionals that follow, we will learn more about the purpose, nature, and design of the man as he was created in the image of God and as he relates to the woman. These are God's ideal purposes for men and women, which we desire to move toward. However, we must keep in mind that entering into God's purposes will be a continual process of learning and transformation. Therefore, we need to be patient with ourselves. We are starting where we are now—not at the place we should be, and not at the place at which we will arrive.

In regard to our spiritual growth, Paul taught us that we are to forget the things that are behind us and reach for what is ahead of us. We are to press on to the mark, which is the *"high calling of God in Christ Jesus"* (Philippians 3:14 KJV). When Jesus came to earth, He showed us the mark that we are to hit. So whatever He says is what we're supposed to pursue. He showed us God's original plan so that we could have something to aim at. We should never accept what we currently have as the norm. Even though it may be the current trend, if it's not what God intended, it's abnormal. We should never live so below our privilege that we begin to believe a lie and call it truth.

When men and women gain an understanding of their uniqueness and purpose in God, they will be able to assist one another in properly understanding and fulfilling the lives God created us to live. They will then also be able to live in right relationship with God, and in the freedom and blessings He planned for us in creation. What's more, when we mend the broken relationships between male and female, both of whom are created in the image of God, we will begin to see healing and new purpose for the individuals, communities, and nations of our world.

⌒

*Thought*: Becoming what God has purposed for us is an act of worship to our Creator.

*Readings*: Psalm 95:1–7; Philippians 3:7–16

# —Day 12—
## GOOD VERSUS BEST

*"'I have the right to do anything,' you say—but not everything is beneficial. 'I have the right to do anything'—but not everything is constructive."* —1 Corinthians 10:23

Wouldn't it be sad to be serious and committed and faithful—to the wrong thing? It would be terrible to be busy doing the wrong things your entire life. It is possible to do good things but not the things that are best based on God's purposes for you.

There are many good people who are pursuing relationships, careers, and goals in life that are not best for them. What we have to concern ourselves with is living effectively.

God created each of us with a purpose that is right for us. Suppose Jesus had become a priest in the Sanhedrin, the highest council and tribunal of the Jews. That would have been a good thing. Suppose He had become a member of the Pharisees and been one of the leaders in the social structure of Galilee and Judea. That would have been a good thing. Suppose He had become a social worker, helping the poor, feeding multitudes of people every day with bread and fish. Would that have been a good thing? Of course. Suppose He had devoted every hour to healing the sick and raising the dead. That would have been a good thing, wouldn't it? Yet none of these things would have been the right thing for Him in fulfilling His chief purpose of being the Savior of humanity.

Jesus was always able to say, in effect, "I know the purpose for My life. Don't distract Me with things that are merely good. I must pursue the highest purpose."

Discovering our purpose enables us to stop wasting our lives and start fulfilling our potential. We must be careful not to become sidetracked along the way. The greatest way to destroy someone is to distract that person from his or her true purpose.

In the Old Testament, Nehemiah fulfilled an important purpose in life, but he might have been sidetracked. He was a Hebrew in exile serving as cupbearer to the king of Persia when he heard that Jerusalem was in a broken-down condition. He was distressed over this, and he determined, "I've got to repair the city." So he prayed, and he obtained permission from the king to rebuild the wall of Jerusalem. God's favor was on his plans because this was the purpose for which he had been created. He went and started to rebuild the wall with the help of the remnant of Jews in Jerusalem.

Some men near Jerusalem didn't like what Nehemiah was doing, and they tried to stop him. Yet Nehemiah told them, "*I am carrying on a great project and cannot go down. Why should the work stop while I leave it and go down to you?*" (Nehemiah 6:3). In the same way, don't allow yourself to be distracted from your primary purpose in God!

⌒

*Thought*: Discovering our purpose enables us to stop wasting our lives and start fulfilling our potential.

*Readings*: Nehemiah 6:1–15; Galatians 6:7–9

# THE GOLD INSIDE YOU

*"I praise you because I am fearfully and wonderfully made;
your works are wonderful, I know that full well."*
—Psalm 139:14

In the mid-twentieth century, in Bangkok, Thailand, the government wanted to build a large highway through a village. In the path of the planned road was a Buddhist monastery with a little chapel, so they had to relocate the monastery—including a heavy, eleven-foot clay statue of Buddha—to another place. When the workers transported the statue of Buddha to the new location and began to lower it into place, unexpectedly, the clay on the statue started to crumble and fall off. The people were afraid because this was a precious religious symbol to them, and they didn't want it to be destroyed. Suddenly, the workers stared in amazement because, as the clay fell away, they saw that the statue was pure gold underneath! Before the statue was moved, people thought it was worth about fifty thousand dollars. Today, that golden Buddha is worth millions and, because of the story behind it, is visited by hundreds of thousands of people every year.

This story illustrates that what we can see is not necessarily what really is. I believe that many of us are living as clay vessels when, in reality, we are pure gold inside. This gold is the dreams we have—or once had—for our lives that are not yet reality, the God-given gifts and talents that we have not yet developed, the purpose for our lives that is not yet fulfilled. How do you remove the clay and uncover the gold within you? Your dreams, talents, and desires can be refined in a process of discovering and fulfilling your life's vision so that the pure gold of your unique and personal gifts to this world can truly shine forth.

Father, You have created me with unique and precious gifts, like gold. Help me to discover these gifts and use them to bless the world around me. In Jesus's name, amen.

*Thought*: Many of us are living as clay vessels when we are pure gold inside.

*Readings*: Psalm 139:1–16; 1 Peter 2:9–10

# —Day 14—
## DON'T GIVE UP ON A PURPOSEFUL LIFE

*"I will repay ["restore to"* NKJV*] you for the years the locusts have eaten."* —Joel 2:25

Are you still questioning what your life is about? I know it's not easy to take a hard look at yourself, but it's necessary if you're going to discover your true purpose in life. You will be busy doing meaningful work when you learn why you are here. Even at twelve years of age, Jesus was busy with His purpose. (See Luke 2:41–49.) Isn't that an exciting way to live? Don't give up on having a purposeful life, no matter what your age. Get busy with the right thing.

I don't have a "job" anymore, but I used to. I worked for the Bahamas government for twelve years. I taught junior high school for five years. I worked in a food store before that, packing shelves. I worked in a warehouse, lifting boxes. I worked in an ad firm, doing advertisements, drawings, and so forth. These were learning experiences. Then I found my true work of helping others understand how to manifest their God-given leadership potential. I don't wake up in the morning and "go" to work. I wake up and become what God created me to be.

Jesus said, *"Let your light so shine before men, that they may see your good works, and glorify your Father which is in heaven"* (Matthew 5:16 KJV). When other people see your work, when they see you manifesting what God put into you, they will glorify God. You were born to do something so awesome that only God could get the credit for it.

God desires that all people find their purpose and fulfill it. I once spoke about purpose at a church in Baton Rouge, Louisiana. A woman came up to me after the service and said, "I'm fifty-six years old, brother. Where were you fifty-six years ago?" I asked, "What do you mean?" She replied, "You're the first person ever to come into my life and help me understand that I have a reason for living—and I can't give an account for fifty-six years right now."

Sometimes, people begin to feel the way that woman did; they're distressed because they've wasted so much time. If this is your situation, don't be discouraged. One of the wonderful things about God is that He has a way of restoring the years that the locusts have eaten. (See Joel 2:23–26.) When you go to Him, He knows how to make up for the time that you've lost.

Yet God would prefer that we follow Him and know our purpose all our lives. That is why the Word of God says very strongly to young people, *"Remember your Creator in the days of your youth"* (Ecclesiastes 12:1). God wants you to remember the Manufacturer early so that He can set you on course for your entire life.

We have only one life, and we have to make that life count if we are ever to fulfill our purpose. Remember, a God-given purpose can be accomplished only through His guidance and strength. *"Now to him who is able to do immeasurably more than all we ask or imagine, according to his power that is at work within us"* (Ephesians 3:20).

⌒

*Thought:* You were born to do something so awesome that only God could get the credit for it.

*Readings:* Psalm 27:7–14; Ephesians 3:14–21

# PURPOSE DIRECTS YOUR PRAYER LIFE

*"Your kingdom come, your will be done, on earth as it is in heaven."* —Matthew 6:10

Praying does not mean convincing God to do your will, but doing His will through your will. Therefore, the key to effective prayer is understanding God's purpose for your life, the reason you exist—as a human being in general and as an individual specifically. This is an especially important truth to remember: once you understand your purpose, it becomes the "raw material," the foundational matter, for your prayer life. God's will is the authority of your prayers. Prayer calls forth what God has already purposed and predestined—continuing His work of creation and carrying out His plans for the earth.

> *In him we were also chosen, having been predestined according to the plan of him who works out everything in conformity with the purpose of his will.* (Ephesians 1:11)

The Father works out everything *"in conformity with the purpose of his will."* In this way, your purpose in God is the foundational material for your prayers regarding provision, healing, deliverance, power, protection, endurance, patience, authority, faith, praise, thanksgiving, confidence, assurance, boldness, and peace, for the supply of all your needs.

Some people say they do not know what to pray for. The answer is that we are not to ask God for anything outside of our purpose. *"When you ask, you do not receive, because you ask with wrong motives, that you may spend what you get on your pleasures"* (James 4:3). If we ask for what is contrary to our purpose, we will be frustrated. Jesus always prayed for God's will to be done, then worked to accomplish it.

Everything you need is available to fulfill your purpose. All that God is, and all that He has, may be received through prayer. The measure of our appropriation of God's grace is determined by the measure of our prayers.

Father, I do not want to accomplish my will, but Your will. Lead me to conform my prayers and myself to the purpose of Your will. In Jesus's name, amen.

*Thought*: Purpose is the raw material for your prayer life.

*Readings*: Daniel 2; 2 Thessalonians 1:11–12

# —Day 16—
## CREATED IN HIS IMAGE

*"So God created man in his own image, in the image of God he created him; male and female he created them."*
—Genesis 1:27 (niv84)

To be a man of purpose and power, it's essential to understand the foundations of God's purposes for both men and women on earth. Mankind was made in the image of God. When God made humanity, He essentially drew man out of Himself so that the essence of man would be just like Him. Since *"God is spirit"* (John 4:24), He created man as spirit. Spirit is eternal. Mankind was created as an eternal being because God is eternal.

It is important to recognize that we are not yet talking about male and female. It was *mankind* that God created in His image. Again, man is spirit, and spirits have no gender. The Bible never talks about a male or female spirit.

What was the reason God created mankind in His image? He didn't create any of the animals or plants in His image. He didn't even make angels in His image. Man is the only being of God's creation that is like Him.

God created mankind for relationship with Himself—to be His family, His offspring, spiritual children of God. It is the nature of God to love and to give. He wanted a being who could be the object of His love and grace. He wanted man to be the recipient of all that He is and all that He has.

The fact that mankind was created in God's image is an awesome revelation about our relationship to Him. God desired children who would be like Himself. Yet He didn't just desire it and then walk away without doing anything about it. He conceived His desire and made it a reality.

In the New Testament, Jesus both affirmed and exemplified God's love for us. He said, *"For God so loved the world that He gave His only begotten Son"* (John 3:16 NKJV). *"He gave."* He gave because He loved. You cannot love without giving. When you love, you give. It's automatic. Yet in order to give love in a way that is truly fulfilling, the receiver has to be like the giver in nature; otherwise, the love would not be complete. You cannot give in a meaningful way to something that is not like you, because it cannot receive your gift in a way that will satisfy your giving. Giving is only complete when the receiver and the giver are alike. God desired a shared and mutual love, not a one-sided love.

*Thought*: When God made man, He essentially drew man out of Himself so that the essence of man would be just like Him.

*Readings*: Genesis 1:26–28; Acts 17:24–28

# CREATED FOR LOVE

*"We love because [God] first loved us."*     —1 John 4:19

We continue to explore the theme of how God created man as spirit so that He and man could share fellowship. The ultimate purpose behind the creation of "man"—both male and female— was love. The Scripture tells us that *"God is love"* (1 John 4:8, 16). What I especially like about this statement is that God doesn't just give love, He doesn't just show love—He *is* love. He desires to share His love with us because love is His essential quality.

God has many other qualities besides love that we could list. He is righteous, holy, omnipotent, and almighty. He is all of these wonderful things and so many more. God could be all of these other attributes and still exist by Himself in isolation. However, it is the nature of love to give of itself, and it cannot give in isolation. In order for love to be fulfilled, it has to have someone to love, and it has to give to its beloved.

*"I am the Lord, and there is no other; apart from me there is no God"* (Isaiah 45:5). There is no other God besides the Lord, yet He is a God of relationship, not isolation. He desires someone of His nature and likeness whom He can love. Therefore, God's primary motivation in the creation of humanity was love. He created men and women because He wanted to share His love with beings like Himself, beings created in His image. This truth is amazing to me!

God looked at what He had created, and here were these beautiful duplicates of Himself to fulfill His love. This is not an abstract concept. This means that the entire human race—including you and me—was created by God to be loved by Him.

We must remember that the only reason we can have this fellowship with God is that He made mankind to be spirit, just as He is Spirit. That is why Jesus tells us that *"God is spirit, and his worshipers must worship in the Spirit and in truth"* (John 4:24).

Although God is our Creator, He has always emphasized that He is also our Father. It wasn't His desire to be primarily thought of by us as an awesome God or a *"consuming fire"* (Deuteronomy 4:24). Although, at times, it is difficult for our religious minds to grasp this concept, God wants us to approach Him as a child would a loving father. *"Let us then approach the throne of grace with confidence, so that we may receive mercy and find grace to help us in our time of need"* (Hebrews 4:16).

God created human beings so that He could have someone to love, someone who would walk with Him and work with Him in His purposes for the earth. That is why, no matter how many relationships you have or how many gifts you buy for others, in the end, you aren't going to be satisfied until you love God. God must have the primary place in your life. Your love was designed to be fulfilled in Him.

⌒

*Thought*: God desires to share His love with us because love is His essential quality.

*Readings*: Psalm 103; 1 John 4:7–21

# — DAY 18 —
## TWO PHYSICAL HOUSES

*"So God created man in his own image, in the image of God
he created him; male and female he created them."*
—Genesis 1:27 (NIV84)

In creation, God placed mankind in two physical houses: male
and female. This means that "man"—the spirit—exists within
every male and every female. The essence of both male and female
is the resident spirit within them, called "man." This fact is often
overlooked, so I want to repeat it: according to the Bible, all
people—males and females alike—are man. Genesis 5:1–2 says,
*"When God created man, he made him in the likeness of God. He
created them male and female and blessed them. And when they were
created, **he called them** [together] 'man'"* (NIV84).

Why did God take man, who is spirit, and put him in two
separate physical entities rather than just one? It was because He
wanted man to fulfill two distinct purposes. We'll explore the
significance of this fact in later devotionals. For now, we need to
remember that the spirit-man has no gender and that, in order
to fulfill His eternal purposes, God used two physical forms to
express the spiritual being made in His image.

In the Bible, when God speaks to humanity, He uses the term
*man*. He doesn't address the male or the female unless He's talking
to individuals. Instead, He talks to the man within them both.
He addresses the spirit-man. God deals with our inner being.
(See Ephesians 3:16.) Many of us are preoccupied by the outward
manifestation of male or female, when we should be focusing first
on the spirit-man. Paul said in Galatians 3:28 that in the body of
Christ there is neither male nor female, neither slave nor master.

Thus, the person who lives inside you—the essential you—is the spirit-man. Although males and females have differences, they are of the same essence. Since human beings fellowship with God and worship Him through their spirits, this means that men and women both have direct spiritual access to God and are individually responsible to Him.

*Thought*: God used two physical forms to express the spiritual being made in His image.

*Readings*: Genesis 5:1–2; Galatians 3:26–29

# A PLACE OF GOD'S CONTINUAL PRESENCE

*"You will fill me with joy in your presence."* —Psalm 16:11

God chose a special place on the planet and put His anointing on it for the sake of man, whom He had created. First Adam, and then Eve, as well, was placed in a delightful environment—a little spot of heaven on earth. (See Genesis 2:8.)

A central reason that God placed Adam and Eve in the garden of Eden was so that they could be in His presence all the time. They could walk and talk with the Lord in the cool of the day. They could hear His voice. This was a place where communion, fellowship, and oneness with God were always intact.

A manufacturer will always position a part in the location where it can best carry out its purpose. God, as our Maker, chose the best possible location and plan for mankind. We can conclude from what we've learned about the environment of the garden that the primary purpose of man is to be in God's presence. Man is not wired to function outside the presence of the Lord.

Here's the significance: God never intended for Adam and Eve to move from the garden. He intended for *the garden to move over the earth.* God wanted them to take the presence of the garden and spread it throughout the world. This is what He meant when He told Adam and Eve to have dominion over the earth. (See Genesis 1:26–28.) This is still God's purpose. As it says in Isaiah 11:9, *"The earth will be full of the knowledge of the Lord as the waters cover the sea"* (NIV84). Adam and Eve could fulfill this purpose only if they were in constant communion with the God of the garden.

Likewise, to live in your purpose, you must make a decision to develop a consistent and deep relationship with God through

Christic. *"Make every effort to be found spotless, blameless and at peace with him.... Grow in the grace and knowledge of our Lord and Savior Jesus Christ"* (2 Peter 3:14, 18).

———

*Thought*: God didn't intend for Adam and Eve to move from the garden. He intended for the garden to move over the earth.

*Readings*: Psalm 89:1–18; 1 Thessalonians 5:16–24

# —DAY 20—
## KNOW YOUR IDENTITY

*"But when he, the Spirit of truth, comes, he will guide you into all the truth."*                              —John 16:13

Jesus was given to prayer and reflection during His entire earthly life. He was in constant contact with the Father in order to know how to fulfill His life's purpose. After a day of particularly busy ministry in which He had healed the sick and demon-possessed, He got up early the next day and went to pray in a quiet place. When Peter and the other disciples found Him there, they exclaimed, *"Everyone is looking for you!"* (Mark 1:37).

Jesus could have basked in the people's praise, but He continued to follow His life's purpose. God had shown Him the next step when He was in prayer. He said, *"Let us go somewhere else—to the nearby villages—so I can preach there also. That is why I have come"* (Mark 1:38).

Until you can hear the voice of God, you will be hindered in becoming a man of purpose and power. You aren't fulfilling your purpose until you start speaking and affirming His Word in your life. To do this, you need to be in the same "garden environment" that Adam and Eve were first placed in.

We need to get back to the place where the glory can flow between God and man, where we can hear the voice of God, and God can give us direction. Because the Holy Spirit has been poured out into the hearts of believers, the garden is no longer just one spot on the earth—it is within the heart of every person who belongs to Christ. That is why Christ said, *"The kingdom of God is within you"* (Luke 17:21 NKJV, KJV). It is not within you of its own accord; the kingdom of God is within you because God's Spirit lives within you.

The kingdom of God—God's Spirit and will ruling in our hearts—has come to us through Christ, and it is through Him that we can fulfill the dominion mandate. We are called to spread the gospel message of reconciliation with God through Christ and of the gift of the Holy Spirit, who brings us power for living, working, and creating to the glory of God. If we want to fulfill our dominion responsibilities and assignments, we have to do so through the Spirit of God as we follow His will.

*Thought*: You aren't fulfilling your purpose until you can hear the voice of God and affirm His Word in your life.

*Readings*: Isaiah 11:1–5; John 14:15–26

# CREATED TO EXHIBIT GOD'S NATURE

*"The spirit of man is the candle of the Lord."*
—Proverbs 20:27 (KJV)

Aprimary reason God created Adam and Eve was so that they could be in relationship with Him and continually remain in His presence. A second essential reason was so that they could reflect His character and personality. Two foundational aspects of God's character are *love* and *light*, and man (male and female) is designed to exhibit these qualities.

Man was always meant to reveal God's nature in the context of being continually connected to Him in fellowship. Jesus spoke of that connection when He referred to Himself as the Vine and us as the branches: *"I am the vine; you are the branches. If you remain in me and I in you, you will bear much fruit; apart from me you can do nothing"* (John 15:5). First John 4:16 says, *"Whoever lives in love lives in God, and God in them,"* and Proverbs 20:27 says, *"The spirit of man is the candle of the Lord"* (KJV). This means that when you have fellowship with God, you reflect His light. You show the nature of God, for *"God is light; in him there is no darkness at all"* (1 John 1:5).

A third reason for the creation of humanity was so that men and women could share God's authority. *"Let us make man in our image,…and let them rule ["have dominion" NKJV, KJV]"* (Genesis 1:26 NIV84). God never wanted to rule by Himself. Love doesn't think in those terms. You can always tell a person who is full of love. They don't want to do anything for their purposes alone. A selfish person wants all the glory, all the credit, all the recognition, all the attention, all the power, all the authority, all the rights, and all the privileges. But a person of love wants others to share in what they have.

Note again that the word *"man"* in Genesis 1:26 refers to the spirit-being created in God's image. The purpose of dominion was given to man *the spirit*. This was before the creation of male and female. Therefore, spiritually, both male and female have the same responsibility toward the earth because rule was given to the spirit-man, which resides in both of them.

Man has been given the freedom to exhibit creativity while governing the physical earth and all the other living things that dwell in it. The earth is to be ruled over, taken care of, fashioned, and molded by beings made in the image of their Creator. In this way, man is meant to reflect the loving and creative Spirit of God.

God also created man to demonstrate His wisdom and the goodness of His precepts. This purpose is part of God's eternal plans: *"His intent was that now, through the church, the manifold wisdom of God should be made known to the rulers and authorities in the heavenly realms, according to his eternal purpose that he accomplished in Christ Jesus our Lord"* (Ephesians 3:10–11).

A man of purpose and power exhibits all of these aspects as he relies on God's Spirit to guide and enable him.

*Thought*: Spiritually, both male and female have the same responsibility toward the earth.

*Readings*: Psalm 100; John 15:5–17

# CREATED TO BE GOD'S CHILDREN

*"Giving joyful thanks to the Father, who has qualified you to share in the inheritance of his holy people in the kingdom of light."* —Colossians 1:12

When God created men and women to share His authority, it was in the context of their relationship to Him as His offspring. God didn't create us to be servants but to be children who are involved in running the "family business." This was His plan for mankind from the beginning. He has always wanted His children to help Him fulfill His purposes.

This means that God doesn't want us to work *for* Him; He wants us to work *with* Him. The Bible says that we are *"God's co-workers"* (2 Corinthians 6:1), or *"workers together with him"* (KJV). In the original Greek, *"co-workers"* means those who "cooperate," who "help with," who "work together."

It's common to hear people say, "I'm working for Jesus." If you are working *for* Jesus, you are still a hired hand. But when you understand the family business, then you become a worker alongside Christ.

What are some of the implications of our being God's children, working in His business? First, we don't have to worry about our day-to-day living expenses. If your father and mother owned a prosperous business, and they put you in charge of it, should you wonder where you will get food to eat? Should you wonder where you will get water to drink? Should you wonder where you will get clothes to wear? No, you are family, and you are going to be provided for. In God's company, there's always plenty of provision to go around, and you can rely on that with confidence.

Second, the Lord's directive to the male and female was, *"Fill the earth and subdue it"* (Genesis 1:28). He was telling them, in essence, "Have dominion over this spot right here so that you become used to ruling on a smaller scale at first." The implication is that He intended for this man and woman to grow in dominion ability by learning to dominate the garden of Eden, the area in which they were initially placed. This is one of God's clear principles: if you've been faithful over a little, then your rulership will be expanded to much more.

Jesus explained this concept clearly in the parable of the talents. To the servant who has been faithful over a little, the master says, *"Well done, good and faithful servant! You have been faithful with a few things; I will put you in charge of many things. Come and share your master's happiness!"* (Matthew 25:23).

God is so good to us. He doesn't give us more than we can handle. He always gives us just enough to train us for the rest. I hope you understand this principle. God will always give you just enough so that you can get used to the idea of more. Many of us want everything right now. We short-circuit God's plan because we grasp for everything at once. God is saying, in effect, "You'll get everything, but not right at this moment. You have not yet developed the character and the experience and the exercising of your potential to enable you to handle more."

*Thought*: God always gives us just enough to train us for the rest.

*Readings*: Exodus 19:3–6; Matthew 25:14–30

# —Day 23—
## GIVING AND RECEIVING

*"For man is not from woman, but woman from man. Nor was man created for the woman, but woman for the man."*
—1 Corinthians 11:8–9 (NKJV)

Males and females were created both similarly and differently in order to fulfill God's purposes. Just as God drew mankind from Himself, creating humans as spiritual beings, He drew the woman out of the man and made her a physical being. This parallel in creation illustrates the oneness and mutual love that God and man, and male and female, were created to have.

The male is essentially a "giver." He is designed to give to the woman. As we discuss further in part three of this devotional, God designed the male to gain satisfaction from both working and providing. When he's able to do these two things, he's a happy man.

Built into the man's desire to work and provide is his need to give. Being a provider can sometimes be just a role for some men, but giving is a function related to a male's design and need. If you want to undermine a man's nature, then provide for him instead of letting him provide. For example, when a wife tells her husband he doesn't need to buy her groceries, that she doesn't need him to do anything for her anymore, she's dealing a blow to an essential part of his being.

If a woman is educated and has a good job, she needs to be careful. She may be tempted to say—or at least to imply—to her husband, "I don't need you or anything you have. You're lucky I married you." She doesn't know how this affects him. The man is designed to be a provider; therefore, no matter how much money a woman earns, she needs to make sure she keeps encouraging him as a provider and then let him bless her with what he gives her.

While the man is essentially a "giver," the woman is essentially a "receiver." If you look at the way the female body is made, she is a receiver from A to Z. She receives seed into her physical, emotional, psychological, and spiritual wombs, incubates it, and makes it something greater than she was originally given. Her receiving complements the male's giving. The woman is of the same essence as the man because the receiver has to be like the giver. However, in order for the woman to be the receiver, she also has to be different from the man.

These differences are complementary in nature and are designed so that the male and female can fulfill one another's emotional and physical needs while they are spiritually nourished by God and His love—and so that, together, they can fulfill their mandate to have dominion over the world.

❧

*Thought*: Men and women were created with complementary designs that reflect their individual roles in fulfilling the larger purposes for which they were created.

*Readings*: Genesis 2:22–24; 1 Corinthians 11:8–9, 11–12

# — DAY 24 —
## THE SOURCE OF CONFLICT

*"Each person is tempted when they are dragged away by their own evil desire and enticed. Then, after desire has conceived, it gives birth to sin; and sin, when it is full-grown, gives birth to death."* —James 1:14–15

If Adam and Eve were created to be in fellowship with God and one another, what happened to change this? Genesis 3 explains the initial source of the conflict between men and women. The devil, in the form of a serpent, tempted the first woman, Eve, to eat what God had forbidden her—and Adam—to eat. (See Genesis 2:16–17.) Personally, I don't think this was the first time the serpent had approached her. First, she didn't seem surprised to see him or to hear him speaking. Second, I believe they had talked earlier about God's instructions because of the way the devil phrased his crafty question: *"Did God **really** say, 'You must not eat from any tree in the garden'?"* (Genesis 3:1). He wanted to cast doubt on Eve's understanding of what God had said.

Eve replied, *"We may eat fruit from the trees in the garden, but God did say, 'You must not eat fruit from the tree that is in the middle of the garden, and you must not touch it, or you will die'"* (verses 2–3). She had most of her information correct, so the devil's next ploy was to try to undermine God's integrity in her eyes. *"'You will not certainly die,' the serpent said to the woman. 'For God knows that when you eat of it your eyes will be opened, and you will be like God, knowing good and evil'"* (verses 4–5).

Eve succumbed to the temptation, Adam joined her of his own free will, and they both ate of the fruit of the tree. (See verse 6.) This decision to reject God's purposes resulted in the spiritual

deaths of the man and the woman. It was the beginning of the conflict between man and God and men and women that we are still
dealing with today. But God had a plan of restoration.

Thought: The devil's first tactic against human beings was to cast
doubt on what God had said.

Readings: Genesis 3:1–7; James 1:12–18

# —Day 25—
# LOSING THE GARDEN

*"So the* Lord *God banished him from the Garden of Eden to work the ground from which he had been taken."*
—Genesis 3:23

Adam and Eve went against God's commandment. It was the spirit-man—the responsible spiritual being—within both the male and female that made the fateful choice to eat the fruit in disobedience to God's command. This is why mankind's ultimate dilemma is a spiritual one.

When Adam and Eve rebelled, they immediately died a spiritual death—just as God had warned—and eventually the physical houses God had given them to live in on the earth also died. However, the spiritual death was the worse predicament of the two because it separated them from their former perfect fellowship with God. God still loved them, but they no longer had the same open channel to Him with which to receive His love. While they still retained elements of their creation in God's image, they no longer perfectly reflected the nature and character of their Creator.

The devil had presented Adam and Eve with a big lie, and they had fallen for it, to their own sorrow. However, there was an underlying reason that mankind fell. To understand it, we need to return to two foundational principles of purpose: (1) To discover the purpose of something, never ask the creation; ask the creator. (2) We find our purpose only in the mind of our Maker. Adam and Eve stopped looking to their Creator for their purpose and instead looked to themselves. In doing so, they lost their ability to fulfill their true purpose.

In the broken relationship between Adam and Eve and the cursed ground that followed their sin (see Genesis 3:14–19), we see Satan's scheme to undermine God's purposes of dominion. Satan was afraid of the power that would be released through a man and woman united in God's purposes. Therefore, he sought to distort the relationship between males and females and limit the garden of Eden by bringing an atmosphere of thorns and thistles to the rest of the earth.

Yet, even though Adam and Eve fell, God's purpose for humanity has never changed. At the very hour of humanity's rejection of His purpose, God promised a Redeemer who would save men and women from their fallen state and all its ramifications. (See Genesis 3:15.) The Redeemer would restore the relationship and partnership of males and females. Jesus Christ is that Redeemer, and, because of Him, men and women can return to God's original design for them. We can fulfill His purposes once again. We can have true dominion over the earth—but only through Christ.

⌒

*Thought*: Satan was afraid of the power that would be released through a man and woman united in God's purposes.

*Readings*: Genesis 3:8–24; Romans 5:12–21

# LIFE IS PRECIOUS

*"Above all else, guard your heart, for everything you do flows from it."* —Proverbs 4:23

When Adam and Eve turned their backs on God and His ways, they ended up losing their knowledge of His intent for themselves and for the world. Rejecting God was the equivalent of buying a sophisticated and intricate piece of equipment and then throwing away the user's manual. If you get something to work under those circumstances, it is only by chance. The more likely scenario is that you will never get it to function properly. It will never fulfill its complete purpose.

Likewise, humanity has not respected the fact that God's creation and His directions for living were established for a specific reason. If that purpose continues to be abandoned, men and women will never function properly as human beings. This dangerous situation leads to us back to one of the key principles for understanding life and relationships: *whenever purpose is not known, abuse is inevitable.*

Life is too valuable to be treated like a trial run. It's a dangerous thing for us to experiment with this precious commodity. In the Psalms, we are reminded that God's Manual, the Word, directs our way: *"Your word is a lamp for my feet, a light on my path"* (Psalm 119:105). *"Your statutes are my heritage forever; they are the joy of my heart"* (verse 111). *"The unfolding of your words gives light; it gives understanding to the simple"* (verse 130). If we look to ourselves or others, rather than to God and His Manual, to learn our reason for living, we will travel an unreliable and hazardous course in life.

What value do you place on your life? Do you know that one of the most dangerous things in life is wasting time? It is said that time is a commodity that you never are able to recapture. Once you've lost time, it's gone forever. So the best thing to do with time is to use it in a way that will bring the greatest results. The best way—the only way—to use time effectively is to do *what* you are supposed to do *when* you are supposed to do it. Effectiveness does not mean just doing good things but rather doing the *right* thing.

*Thought*: You have to make your life count if you are ever to fulfill your purpose.

*Readings*: Proverbs 4:18–27; Hebrews 4:12–16

— DAY 27 —

# RESTORED BY REDEMPTION

*"For he has rescued us from the dominion of darkness and brought us into the kingdom of the Son he loves, in whom we have redemption, the forgiveness of sins."*
—Colossians 1:13–14

Jesus Christ restored humanity to God's purpose and plan. I define the plan of God very simply. The first two chapters of Genesis are a depiction of God's perfect program for the spirit-man and his manifestation as male and female. Chapter 3 of Genesis reveals how and why this program fell apart. Genesis 3 to Revelation 21, the last chapter of the Bible, explain what God has done and is still doing to restore humanity to His original program (and even beyond). The Bible is an account of God's restoration program, which He effected through various covenants with His people.

Christ's life, death, and resurrection accomplished the redemption of man. The sacrifice of the perfect Man made atonement for the sins of fallen man and restored humanity to the fellowship with God it had enjoyed in the garden of Eden. This means that the curse of sin is removed from people's lives when they receive Christ's redemptive work and are born again. Christ's own Spirit comes to dwell within them, they are restored to God's purposes, and they are able to love and serve God again.

Under the redemptive work of Christ, the woman is restored not only to fellowship with God, but also to the position of partner with her male counterpart. Therefore, she is not to be dominated or ruled by the male, because, if she were, it would mean that the redemptive work of Christ had not been successful.

Jesus said, "*When the Advocate* [Holy Spirit] *comes, whom I will send to you from the Father—the Spirit of truth who goes out from the Father—he will testify about me. And you also must testify, for you have been with me from the beginning*" (John 15:26–27). From the Father *through* the Son *by* the Spirit, we are taught the truth, which we, in turn, teach others. This is part of man's dominion assignment carried out by redeemed men and women. The only instruction we are supposed to speak comes from the Father. The Father, through Jesus, gives instructions by the Holy Spirit to the bride, the church. Then the church takes the instructions from her Lord and speaks them out with authority as commands. This is the principle behind Jesus's statements to believers regarding authority. He has given His bride, the church, the authority to use His name to command sickness, disease, demons, and mountains. (See Luke 9:1–2; Matthew 17:20; Mark 16:17–18.)

As the bride of Christ, the church has the Father's instruction, authority, and power to speak and act with boldness in the world. The church binds, looses, heals, and delivers under the authority of our Teacher and Husband, Jesus Christ. (See, for example, Matthew 16:19.)

*Thought*: Jesus Christ restored humanity to God's purpose and plan.

*Readings*: Psalm 107; Revelation 5:9–10

# —DAY 28—
## THE FOUNDATION OF SOCIETY
## AND THE FAMILY

*"The LORD God formed a man from the dust of the ground and breathed into his nostrils the breath of life, and the man became a living being."* —Genesis 2:7

When you think about it, God really made only one human being. When He created the female, He didn't go back to the soil, but He fashioned her from the side of the man. (See Genesis 2:21–23.) Only the male came directly from the earth. This was because the male was designed by God to be the foundation of the human family. The woman came out of the man rather than the earth because she was designed to rest on the man—to have the male as her support.

God planned everything before He created it, and He started with the foundation. Have you ever seen a contractor build a house starting with the roof? No. Likewise, you don't start with the windows. You don't start with the gutters or the rafters. God starts like any other builder. The priority in building is always what you need to do first. You begin with the foundation.

I believe that the foundation of society, the infrastructure God intended for this world, has been misunderstood. We often say that the family is the foundation of society. It is very true that the family is the adhesive that holds it together. Yet God did not start to build earthly society with a family. He began it with one person. He began it with the male.

Yet we must remember that even though the male is the foundation of society and the family, men and women were created equal. *"In Christ Jesus you are all children of God through faith....*

There is neither Jew nor Gentile, slave nor free, nor is there male and female, for you are all one in Christ Jesus" (Galatians 3:26, 28). Men and women are equal. That's not for a senate or a congress or a cabinet or a parliament of any nation to decide. God already made this decision in creation! Then He reaffirmed it with the redemption of mankind in Jesus Christ. Male and female are one in Christ.

Thought: While the male is the foundation of society and the family, men and women were created equal.

Readings: Genesis 2:4–23; 1 Corinthians 11:3, 7–12

— DAY 29 —

# THE IDENTITY CRISIS

*"Your Father knows the things you have need of before you ask Him."*　　　　　　　　　　　　—Matthew 6:8 (NKJV)

The greatest challenge for men today, especially young men, is that they suffer from an identity crisis. They lack the nurturing influence of a true father to give them identity. An identity doesn't come from a gang or the government. It comes from a father.

The only one who can give you your true identity as a man is a father. This fundamental principle is lacking in many of our cultures, and its absence is the source of many social problems. Most young men are running around looking for a father, and they can't find him. They're running to their friends, but to no avail. You can't find fatherhood in another peer or gang member who is also looking for a father. You cannot discover who you are by looking to someone who doesn't know who he or she is.

A man needs to be affirmed by a father in order to confirm his manhood. This is why so many young men yearn to hear their fathers say to them, "I love you, Son. You're a man now." If you haven't found a true earthly father yet, God qualifies as your Father. Hallelujah! You can come to God and say, "God, who am I?" and He'll tell you, "You're My son." *"But as many as received him* [Jesus], *to them gave he power to become the sons of God, even to them that believe on his name"* (John 1:12 KJV). If you have received Jesus, you have the power to become a child of God. Your identity then comes from Him.

Next, God the Father will say to you, "Now, mature into the image of My dear Son, Jesus Christ, and you will grow up in Him until you are a true man." Jesus the Son tells you, "You are a father." He gives you your identity as a father. The principle of fatherhood, therefore, is simple: *you provide identity.* When you receive your true identity in Christ, then you can provide true identity to others.

A male can do nothing greater than fathering—whether he is fulfilling the role of father for his children or for others in his sphere of influence. He can earn a million dollars, but if he fails to fulfill God's calling to father as God fathers, then he is a failure.

Additionally, a male who is physically strong but weak as a father is not a man. A male eloquent in words but silent as a father in teaching his household the Word and precepts of God is not a man. The measure of a man's success is directly related to his effectiveness as a father, for which God is the only true example and standard.

⌒

*Thought*: When you receive your true identity in Christ, then you can provide true identity to others.

*Readings*: Jeremiah 31:7–9; Luke 15:11–32

— DAY 30 —
# THE MALE AS VISIONARY

*"He has also set eternity in the hearts of men."*
—Ecclesiastes 3:11 (NIV84)

While purpose is why you were born, vision is when you start seeing it yourself. God wants men to understand their dominion assignments and then to develop the qualities that are required in order to carry them out. This is the way that men can pursue God's purpose for their lives and grow in true manhood, for God's purpose is the key to our fulfillment.

The first responsibility that brings fulfillment and spiritual rewards to the male is that of visionary. This is a foundational responsibility because, without it, he can't fulfill the other assignments of leader, teacher, cultivator, protector, and provider.

Being a true visionary is a lost art in our times. The average male can't say who he is because he has no real vision for his life. He is either floundering without purpose or he is diligently pursuing a false vision based on the values of contemporary society, which are often the opposite of what God values. God wants males to have a vision for their lives that comes from Him and belongs to them personally—not something dictated by the cultural environment, current trends, man-made religion, or someone else's image of what their lives should be.

We can know that God has a vision for every male because the male was *created* to be a visionary. One reason the man was formed first was so that he could be the initial recipient of the information, revelation, and communication God desired to share regarding humanity's relationship with Him and its purpose for being.

Then He created the female to enable the man to fulfill this vision. God's priority has not changed.

Many men are not living in the purposes God has for them because they are thinking in limited terms. Let me encourage you: your dreams are not crazy; they are your lifework. Staying in a job that is not right for you is like a fish trying to be a horse. That's why you have high blood pressure. That's why there's so much stress in your life. You're doing things you weren't born to do. Stop thinking small. Move into your purpose—not only for your sake, but also for others'.

A woman was created by God to help a man, but the man has to be doing something! God's purpose for creating the female was to help the male with his purpose and assignment. When a man finds his work, a woman finds her assignment. I believe many marriages are breaking up—even in the church—because women are not helping their husbands with the work God has given them. Your wife is waiting for you to find your purpose because her assignment in life is tied to it. She was designed to help you. She may also have her own work, but for her to help you fulfill yours, you have to know your purpose.

Since God designed a female to help a male, everything He put in the female works toward that purpose. That's why a woman is such an amazing creation! She is one mean helping machine! When she shows up in your life, she has everything you need. She has insight, intuition, stamina, wisdom, counsel, the ability to carry burdens, and the capacity to incubate ideas. She can talk about your vision and protect your resources.

Do you understand your purpose in life? Are you thinking in limited terms—or in God's terms?

*Thought:* What are you doing with the dreams God has given you?

*Readings:* Proverbs 18:16; 2 Timothy 1:6–7

# WHERE THERE IS NO VISION

*"Where there is no vision, the people perish."*
—Proverbs 29:18 (KJV)

A man needs a clear vision of three things: (1) who he is in God, (2) what his overall purpose as a male is, and (3) what his purpose as an individual man is. In this way, he can know where he is going in life and can lead those under his care and responsibility. *"Where there is no vision, the people perish."*

Vision is necessary for life. The word *"vision"* in the Hebrew means a "dream, revelation, or oracle." Obviously, a vision that is connected to God's purposes is something that needs to be revealed by God Himself. You need His revelation of your life's vision. The only way you can discover this vision is to listen to what God is saying to you.

To have vision means to be able to conceive of and move toward your purpose in life. A man shouldn't get married and then say to his wife, "What are we going to do? Well, you know, we'll just wait on the Lord. We'll see where we're going when we get there." That's not vision. While God does want us to wait for His guidance and direction, He doesn't want us to abuse this principle by not earnestly seeking His particular vision and plan for us.

Now, it's true that we might not always see the whole picture right away, just as Abraham had to trust God to lead him to an unfamiliar land in which he would become a great nation. (See Genesis 12:1–2.) However, Abraham had a clear vision that he was going to the place God had promised him, and he moved steadily toward that goal. Having vision means that you can already see the end of your purpose. It means that you have faith in God and what

He has told you to do, so that you are continually moving toward your vision as it is moving toward you. Your responsibility is to support and sustain the vision until it comes to fruition.

*Thought*: To have vision means to conceive of and move toward your purpose.

*Readings*: Genesis 12:1–5; Romans 11:29

# SEE THE VISION

*"Now faith is confidence in what we hope for and assurance about what we do not see."* —Hebrews 11:1

The greatest example of someone who had a vision for His life is Jesus. He constantly repeated and affirmed who He was. Jesus knew His identity as the Son of God and as God the Son. He knew His reason for being and His purpose in life. (See, for example, John 8:58; Luke 19:10.)

The example Jesus set for us shows us our need for these important elements related to purpose: (1) a clear self-image and (2) a life consistent with one's purpose and calling. Jesus lived a life that was totally consistent with who He said He was. He had complete integrity; He always kept and fulfilled His own words.

Vision is the capacity to see beyond your physical eyes into a preferred future. Vision is purpose in pictures. Have you been seeing pictures of your dream? Perhaps your dreams are being drowned out by your music, your phone, and other people talking. When you turn off the TV and computer and everything is quiet, do you start thinking of your future? In the Bible, whenever God wanted to speak to someone about their work, He always took them away from other people. God took Abraham to a mountain all by himself. He took Moses to the desert. David heard from God when he was out tending sheep in the hills. You need to disengage from the noise of life so you can see pictures of your future.

Purpose produces a vision, and a vision produces a plan. Once there's a plan, it produces discipline in you. Write down your purpose and vision, and then get some pictures symbolizing that vision and what you need to fulfill it. I cut out pictures of my dream and put them where I could see them every day. I would say, "That's what I'm going to do."

"*Many are the plans in a person's heart, but it is the LORD's purpose that prevails*" (Proverbs 19:21). I want this Scripture to be emblazoned on your heart. God's purpose for your life is already established; He's not worried about your future. Whatever you were born to do is already finished in Him. Cease worrying about it, capture His vision for your life, and start making plans to go there.

It doesn't matter what you currently have or don't have, as long as you can see what you could have. This vision is the key to life because where there's a dream, there's hope, and where there's hope, there's faith—and faith is the substance, or fulfillment, of what you are hoping for. (See Hebrews 11:1.)

I encourage you to believe in your daydreams and to reconnect with your passion; your vision awaits your action. Your future is not ahead of you—it lies within you. See beyond your eyes and live for the unseen. Your vision determines your destiny. God truly has plans for you.

⌒

*Thought*: Capture God's vision for your life and start making plans to go there.

*Readings*: Habakkuk 2:2–3; 2 Timothy 2:20–21

# VISION IS UNSELFISH

*"Do nothing out of selfish ambition or vain conceit. Rather, in humility value others above yourselves, not looking to your own interests but each of you to the interests of the others."*
—Philippians 2:3–4

True vision is unselfish. Its purpose is to bring God's kingdom on earth and turn people to Him. A vision should always focus on helping humanity or building up others in some way.

First, this means that God will never have you pursue your vision at the expense of your family. A beloved friend of mine went to a conference where a supposed prophet spoke to him about what God wanted for his life. He came to me and asked, "Did you hear what the prophet said? What do you think?" I replied, "Well, let's pray over that prophecy. Let's take our time, get counsel, and find God's will on it." However, the next time I heard from him, he had already set up a plan to fulfill this prophecy. He went to another country, leaving behind a confused and angry family. Was this really God's purpose?

There are instances when family members will agree to be apart for a time to serve a certain purpose. Moreover, your family will not always understand or support your dream. Yet pursuing it shouldn't destroy their lives. Vision should always be accompanied by compassion.

Second, a true vision will not take the form of building a big business just so you can have millions of dollars for expensive homes and cars. These things may be goals, but they are not vision—in fact, they are probably selfish ambition because they build your kingdom rather than God's kingdom. Your vision might well involve making a large amount of money. The difference, however, is in your motivation and attitude. You need to treat your finances as a resource God has provided to fulfill your vision, not as a tool to fill your life with luxuries.

I invite you to pray the following prayer:

Father, I know that You want me to pursue my life's dreams with compassion for others. Please keep me from selfish motives. In Jesus's name, amen.

Thought: Vision's purpose is to bring about God's kingdom on earth.

Readings: Proverbs 11:25; James 3:13–18

# — Day 34 —
## IMAGES OF LEADERSHIP

*"I brought you up from the land of Egypt, I redeemed you from the house of bondage; and I sent before you Moses, Aaron, and Miriam."* —Micah 6:4 (NKJV)

When you see the word *leadership*, whose face pops into your mind? Who is your idea of a strong leader?

Most of us have developed our images of leaders from the wrong sources. We have looked to athletes, musicians, movie stars, and politicians as our role models. Yet the majority of these famous men and women don't know what a true leader is. If you don't believe me, ask them where their children are; ask them where their wives and husbands are; ask them how their home lives are. Many of the world's wealthiest, most famous, most prestigious people can't keep their homes together.

We have looked to status and personal accomplishment as the measure of leadership rather than to God's standards. God is concerned with people who have a vision from Him and who can support, sustain, and nurture their families and others in pursuit of God and His purposes.

Some men want to run away from the responsibility of leadership. They look at it as too much of a burden. They let their wives run everything. Others want to pursue their own selfish interests without worrying about the needs of others. Certain men don't think they deserve to be leaders. They think you have to be rich, successful, or highly educated in order to lead.

Let me make something very clear: if you are a male, you were born to lead. God made the male first because He wanted him to be responsible. A male doesn't decide to lead or not to lead. He has his position by virtue of his purpose; it is inherent. In God's plan, that is not a debatable issue.

*Thought*: We have looked to status and personal accomplishment as the measure of leadership rather than to God's standards.

*Readings*: Exodus 18:13–26; 1 Timothy 3:1–13

# — Day 35 —
## STRONG AND COURAGEOUS

*"Be strong and of good courage, do not fear nor be afraid of them; for the LORD your God, He is the One who goes with you. He will not leave you nor forsake you."*
—Deuteronomy 31:6 (NKJV)

A leader has been designed to take risks and meet challenges. God often gives men assignments that seem too big for them—and they are. They can be accomplished only through God's help. Yet the qualities of courage, strength, and daring enable men to take the necessary steps of faith that bring God's intervention.

It is impossible to be the leader of the family and of society if you are not strong and courageous. After Moses died, the Lord said to Joshua, *"Be strong and courageous, because you will lead these people..."* (Joshua 1:6). Joshua had a "family" of three million people to lead! God gave this young Israelite a job designed for a man. God added something to His command to Joshua. He said, "Be careful to obey all the commands." (See Joshua 1:7.)

A strong man has to be submitted to God's authority. No man can be strong if he is not accountable to someone else. A real man doesn't ignore authority. He remains in the garden of God's presence, praying and reading God's Word, so that he may understand and obey His commands. As a man of God, you must realize that you were not put in a leadership position because you are big, strong, or overbearing. You are put in that position because of your purpose. Your strength is meant to support that purpose.

Some men take their courage and strength and use them recklessly. When a man turns from God, takes his life into his own hands, and doesn't combine courage with common sense, he can cause himself and his family many problems. True courage and strength come only through confidence in the faithfulness of God and belief in His Word.

⌒

*Thought*: The qualities of courage, strength, and daring enable men to take the necessary steps of faith that bring God's intervention.

*Readings*: Joshua 1:1–9; Hebrews 11

# —Day 36—
# A SERVANT'S HEART

*"The Son of Man did not come to be served, but to serve, and
to give his life as a ransom for many."*    —Matthew 20:28

A real man, a true leader, is a servant. He is not a ruler. He
takes care of others before himself. Jesus said,

> *You know that the rulers of the Gentiles lord it over them, and
> their high officials exercise authority over them. Not so with
> you. Instead, whoever wants to become great among you must
> be your servant, and whoever wants to be first must be your
> slave—just as the Son of Man did not come to be served, but
> to serve, and to give his life as a ransom for many.*
> (Matthew 20:25–28)

The apostle Paul echoed this theme when he wrote, *"Each of
you should look not only to your own interests, but also to the interests of others"* (Philippians 2:4 NIV84), and *"Husbands, love your
wives, just as Christ loved the church and gave himself up for her"*
(Ephesians 5:25). How did Christ love His church? First of all, by
giving Himself for her. This means that a man should give up his
personal, private, ambitious, egotistical desires in order to serve
his wife and family. He needs to emulate Christ's nature.

A true leader has *humility*, so that he is willing to learn from
others and be corrected when need be. Some of the greatest
moments in my life are times when my wife corrects me, gives me
ideas, or provides insight on something that I haven't been able to
do right. My wife has awesome resources within her. It takes a real
man to submit to help. It takes a fool to avoid it. God is looking for

a leader who makes himself fruitful by being pruned when necessary in order to yield a healthier and greater harvest.

*Thought:* A true leader has humility, so that he is willing to learn from others and be corrected when need be.

*Readings:* 1 Samuel 3:9–11; Philippians 2:5–11

—DAY 37—

# DESIGNED TO WORK

*"The LORD God took the man and put him in the Garden of Eden to work it and take care of ["cultivate" NASB] it."*
—Genesis 2:15

The nature of the work the male was given to do was not mindless labor—it was cultivation. To *cultivate* means to make something grow and produce a greater yield. *Cultivate* also means to make something fruitful, to develop it into its perfection. The man is to be a developer and a fruit producer. Since God gave this assignment to the male before the female was created, and before the first child was born, the purpose of the male is to develop and cultivate both people and things to God's glory.

God Himself worked when He created the world, and He still works to carry out His purposes. Paul said in Philippians 2:13, *"It is God who works in you to will and to act according to his good purpose"* (NIV84). Because you are made in God's image and likeness, you are designed to work. Work is meant to include creativity and cultivation, not drudgery. It is also supposed to be kept in its proper place. In Genesis 2, the Bible says that God worked hard and completed His work, and then He stopped His work and rested. He didn't burn the midnight oil or work seven days a week just for the sake of working. He stopped working when it was appropriate. He told us to do the same. (See Exodus 20:9–10.)

What is the significance of work? First, work exposes a man's potential. You cannot show what you have inside unless demands are made on it, and demands are placed on it by work.

Second, work allows a man to reflect God's nature. God gave the male work because it is related to his purpose. His purpose is to stay in the presence of the Lord and learn to manage what God has given him to do. In this way, he can eventually fulfill God's complete plan for him, which is to have dominion over the earth.

Third, work enables a man to provide for those for whom he is responsible in his position as visionary and leader. *Provide* comes from a Latin word meaning "to see ahead." Again, the male should have a vision for his life, and he should work to see that it is accomplished—for himself, his family, and others under his care.

I once asked God, "Lord, with all the responsibilities You gave us men, how do we know we can fulfill them?" His answer was very, very simple. He said, "Whatever I call for, I provide for." God is the ultimate Provider. He will provide whatever we need to fulfill our responsibilities. *"I can do everything through him who gives me strength"* (Philippians 4:13 niv84).

⟿

*Thought:* Work is meant to include creativity and cultivation, not drudgery.

*Readings:* Genesis 2:8–15; Colossians 3:23–24

# CREATED TO PROTECT

*"Be strong in the Lord and in his mighty power."*
—Ephesians 6:10

The male is like God's "security guard." When he shows up, everyone is supposed to feel protected and safe. Remember that the atmosphere of God's garden is His presence. Therefore, God essentially told Adam, "Protect the garden, but also protect the presence that is in it. Don't let anything disturb My presence here." It is up to males to maintain God's presence—at their homes, jobs, or any other place in society.

A male is a natural protector. His bone structure and upper body strength are designed to defend, protect, and guard. Now, even if a man isn't tall or extremely muscular, he seems to have inner physical resources that enable him to defend. A man's wife should be able to run to him any time trouble comes.

The safest place for a woman should be in the arms of her husband. Yet one of the saddest things I've seen is men abusing their strength. Instead of using it to protect women, they use it to destroy them. When I think of a man hitting a woman, my whole body turns into a boiling pot of indignation. God gave him muscles to protect her, not to hurt her. *"Husbands ought to love their wives as their own bodies"* (Ephesians 5:28).

A man's wife and children are supposed to feel totally at peace in his presence. As soon as he shows up, everything is in order. When they hear his voice, everything is all right. When a daughter gets hurt, her father's presence makes her feel better. When a son goes away to college, becomes homesick, and feels as if his life is falling apart, he can call his father and hear him say, "Son, it's going to be okay." Suddenly, everything comes into place because Dad spoke a reassuring word. When a wife becomes frustrated or emotional about what's happening in the family, her husband can say, "God says He'll be here for us, and I will be here for us, too." That's a man's responsibility.

I hear some men saying, "I can't wait until I get married so I can practice what he's teaching." Don't wait until then. A man doesn't need to be married to be responsible for women. Start being the protector of every female who comes into your presence, because you were created to be responsible for her.

Men, when you are dating, you don't protect a woman by throwing away your own armor. You don't take her for a drive at night and park in a secluded place. Keep the lights on bright. Keep the conversation in God's light. It takes a real man to keep his hands to himself. That's true strength.

Any woman should feel safe with you when you understand that your purpose is to protect and guard her and to lead her into the things of God. What should happen if a woman comes to you destitute, broken, depressed, sad, or vulnerable, and she confides in you? The spirit of protection should come upon you. Lead her straight to God. Show her Jesus. Then exemplify His character by treating her in a fatherly or brotherly way.

*Thought*: A male seems to have inner physical resources that enable him to defend.

*Readings*: Psalm 68:4–5; Ephesians 6:10–18

## — DAY 39 —
# A TRULY STRONG MAN

*"Some trust in chariots and some in horses, but we trust in the
name of the LORD our God."* —Psalm 20:7

Because men have lost the knowledge of what God created them
to be, they often mistake power for strength. Much of a man's tendency to control comes from a false understanding of how his own
nature is to function in dominion.

Men have a deep desire to prove they are strong. It is one of
the underlying issues every male faces, whether he is a ten-year-old
boy or a ninety-year-old man. Men's internal passion to prove their
strength is inherent in their nature. All men have it in some form
or another because of the purpose for which they were created. It
is built in by God in order to give them the ability to fulfill their
purpose of leading, protecting, and providing. The problem is that
the male's passion to prove his strength has been perverted and
abused by Satan and the sinful nature.

Because of this desire to prove their strength, there is nothing more frightening to most men than to be perceived as weak.
Again, this fear is a result of the fall. Men don't want to be thought
of as being helpless or out of control by either males or females.
This fear drives them to feel as if they have to constantly prove
themselves. It is the source of their aggressive spirit and their often
overly competitive nature. It is also the source of some men's tendency toward violence. A lot of men have muscle but are weak in
their minds, their hearts, their discipline, their responsibility, and
their spirits.

Men need a picture of what a truly strong man looks like. A
strong man is a man who understands his God-given strength. To

be a strong man is to maximize all your potential for the purpose for which you were created. Jesus was the strongest Man who ever lived, yet He is also described as meek. Someone has said that meekness is power under control. That is what true strength is. It is power that is ready to be channeled into good and constructive purposes rather than irresponsible or selfish ones.

Males didn't choose their position; God gave it to them. Whenever you take your position by force, you've moved out of your legal standing. The difference between an elected head of state and a dictator is very simple. The first has authority and the second merely has power. To have authority means to have a right to govern. Therefore, if a man slaps his wife, kicks his children, and then says, "I'm the man of the house; I do what I want," that's an abuse of authority; it's merely wielding power over others. Whenever you abuse your power, you no longer have legitimate authority. Any time a man starts to dominate another human being, he is out of God's will.

*Thought*: To be a strong man is to maximize all your potential for the purpose for which you were created.

*Reading*: Micah 6:8; Matthew 5:3–12

# THERE IS A SEASON

*"To everything there is a season, a time for every purpose under heaven."* —Ecclesiastes 3:1 (NKJV)

One of my greatest mentors, Oral Roberts, told me, "Son, if you're going to be successful in life, expect the best and prepare for the worst."

You are not to trust in the permanence of anything on earth except for your relationship with God. Parents, friends, coworkers, pastors, church members—they're all for a season. Be prepared for the season of living without them. We must have our anchor on the Rock because the Rock has no season—He is eternal. *"The eternal God is your refuge, and underneath are the everlasting arms"* (Deuteronomy 33:27).

Even with those who tell you, "The Lord sent me to work with you," you can expect their departure at some point. So, when a staff member comes to me and says, "The Lord told me it's time to move on," I say, "Well, praise God, thank you for your contribution for the last twenty years. Now, what do you need to help you get where you're going?"

To everything there is a season. Suppose your business is going well. Prepare now for what you will do if your business goes through some tough times. Don't panic and say, "God has left me and the devil has taken over." No, that's just a season. Perhaps you don't like your current job. God says, "That's no problem; everything is seasonal." Think in those terms. You have to know how to handle what life brings you. You have to be an anchor that is not driven by every wind and wave.

Ask God to instruct you in His Word through the power of the Holy Spirit. He desires to give us His wisdom, knowledge, and understanding: *"For the* LORD *gives wisdom, and from his mouth come knowledge and understanding"* (Proverbs 2:6 NIV84). *"Get wisdom, get understanding; do not forget my words or swerve from them"* (Proverbs 4:5 NIV84). Jesus said, *"But the Counselor, the Holy Spirit, whom the Father will send in my name, will teach you all things and will remind you of everything I have said to you"* (John 14:26 NIV84).

⟨⟩

*Thought*: You are not to trust in the permanence of anything on earth except for your relationship with God.

*Readings*: Ecclesiastes 1:1–2, 5–6; James 1:2–4

## —DAY 41—
# GOD'S TRAINING CENTER

*"And the LORD God commanded the man…."*
—Genesis 2:16

I hope you are convinced that you need to be in God's purposes in order to be fulfilled in life! What God gave Adam to do still holds true for men today because, as a God of purpose, He has a reason for everything He does. He is teaching us His plan for mankind in the account of creation.

> *The LORD God took the man and put him in the Garden of Eden to work it and take care of it. And the LORD God commanded the man….* (Genesis 2:15–16)

Whom did the Lord command? He commanded the male. What did He tell him? *"You are free to eat from any tree in the garden; but you must not eat from the tree of the knowledge of good and evil, for when you eat of it you will surely die"* (verses 16–17). One of the male's purposes is teacher. God wanted him to be the initial recipient of His plan for mankind. He showed him the whole garden, the whole environment of Eden, a vision of everything He had created, and then He gave him instructions for living.

Recall that the female wasn't formed until after the events of the above Scripture passage. Thus, the male was given the charge of being the visionary and leader, the one who would guide those who came after him in the ways of God. This doesn't mean that women don't also have the capacity to be visionaries and leaders. However, the male is the one to whom God first entrusted His plans and purposes for the world. This indicates a major purpose of his existence.

*Thought*: The male is the one to whom God first entrusted His plans and purposes for the world.

*Readings*: Genesis 2:15–22; Matthew 28:19–20

## BECOMING A WHOLE PERSON

*"Seek first his kingdom and his righteousness, and all these things will be given to you as well."* —Matthew 6:33

Some people are afraid of being unmarried and alone. That's the reason many people marry spouses who aren't right for them. The problem is that they haven't yet learned what it means to be a whole person.

There is a difference between "being alone" and "being lonely." You can be lonely in a crowd of people, and you can be alone and still happy as a lark. There is nothing wrong with being alone at times. The Bible tells us that it's important to be alone and quiet before the Lord. Jesus often made a point to go off by Himself in order to pray and rest. Many people don't have time for God because they're too busy trying to find a mate.

Being alone can be healthy—but loneliness is like a disease. Jesus talked about the attitude we should have when He said, in effect, "Don't worry about what you're going to eat, what you're going to wear, or whom you're going to marry. Seek first the kingdom of God. Become immersed in His righteousness. Then God will meet all your needs." (See Matthew 6:31–33.)

The criteria for marriage is not merely being old enough, but also whether or not it will be beneficial. (See 1 Corinthians 6:12.) If you don't have a clear understanding of the purpose of marriage, it's not going to benefit you. If your potential spouse doesn't have a clear understanding of who he or she is in Christ and who males and females were created to be, it will not be beneficial for you.

We have seen that when a man falls in love with God's presence, he begins to function as he was meant to. The first man,

Adam, was so busy following the command of God that, when his mate, Eve, came along, he was ready, and it was the right time for him. (See Genesis 2:15–25.) Stay in the garden of God's righteousness because if it's His will for you to have a spouse, you will need to understand His ways if you want that relationship to be a good one.

Follow God's purpose and you will avoid heartache and regret in your relationships, because His purpose is the key to your fulfillment.

⌣⌐

*Thought*: Be prepared for meeting your spouse by first understanding and obeying God's ways.

*Readings*: Deuteronomy 10:12–13; Matthew 6:25–33

# — Day 43 —
## A CRISIS OF ROLES

*"Know that the LORD, He is God; it is He who has made us,*
*and not we ourselves."* —Psalm 100:3 (NKJV)

People used to acquire their ideas of manhood and womanhood from observing their fathers and mothers or from longstanding cultural traditions. Yet hundreds, even thousands, of years of tradition have been set aside in just one or two generations. My life is completely different from my father's life. I can't use the way my father did things as a model for myself, and my sisters can't use the environment in which my mother functioned as an example for themselves. Our parents lived not only in a different generation, but also with different concepts of maleness and femaleness. Historically speaking, until recently, the man had certain accepted roles and the woman had certain accepted roles, and they didn't usually overlap.

What makes our current cultural situation unsettling for men, in particular, is that males have traditionally defined their manhood by their roles: the functions they perform for their families and in society. However, there's been a major shift in the roles of both males and females. The rules of society are changing. We're in the middle of a cultural transition, and competing ideas of masculinity are causing perplexing problems for men. They are being pulled in several directions at once while they try to figure out what it means to be a real man in today's world.

Men's basic conceptions of manhood are therefore being disrupted. They feel displaced. They are either frustrated or struggling to adapt to a new but vague concept of who they are, or they're angry and trying to reverse the flow of change.

Are cultural roles to be totally abandoned? If so, what will replace them? Remember, God knew exactly what He wanted when He thought of the male and female. This means that He is the only One who knows how humanity is intended to function. *"Is he not your Father, your Creator, who made you and formed you?"* (Deuteronomy 32:6). If you have any questions about your relationship with your spouse, you should check the Manual. If you don't know the purpose of something, all you can do is experiment. Everybody who doesn't know his or her purpose is just experimenting with life.

Together, males and females are an intentional divine project with a predetermined purpose. Do you know what most marriages are today? Big experiments. Some men think, "I don't really know what a wife is for, but I'm old enough to get married, so I'm going to have one." All right, then what? Do you know what you have? After three weeks, you realize your wife doesn't agree with you on everything. The experiment isn't working. She begins to ask for things like time. She wants love and affection and attention. She wants appreciation. If you are in this situation, you may say, "Hey, I didn't bargain for all that." Well, my friend, marriage is not a trial run. *"'The two will become one flesh'.... So they are no longer two, but one"* (Matthew 19:5–6).

⸻

*Thought*: When God created the male and the female, He had already predetermined what we were supposed to be and do.

*Readings*: Jeremiah 29:11; Ephesians 1:11

— Day 44 —

# THE CHIEF CORNERSTONE

*"Built on the foundation of the apostles and prophets, with Christ Jesus himself as the chief cornerstone."*
—Ephesians 2:20

The male is the foundation, but he is not the Rock. Who is that Rock? It is Jesus Christ.

Many of us aren't familiar with how essential a cornerstone can be to a building; the way we build many of our structures today, what we call the cornerstone is usually just a facade. On one of my trips to Israel, however, I saw a clear example of what it means for Christ to be the Chief Cornerstone of our lives.

I was traveling with a group in the area of Capernaum. We went to visit an ancient synagogue, one that Jesus was said to have taught in. Being very inquisitive, I walked around the little synagogue, and I noticed that, in back, there was a rock at the bottom of the foundation. I asked our guide, who was a Jewish rabbi, "What is that rock?" He replied, "Oh, that is the chief cornerstone."

Thinking of the verse from Ephesians, I said, "Explain that to me." The rabbi said, "They laid foundations by interlocking stones." In other words, they didn't pour concrete in those days; they used interlocking systems. Every rock was carved to fit into the rock next to it so that they locked in place. When the foundation was nearly completed, one stone had to lock into the last two stones in one corner to seal the whole thing together. That was the cornerstone. Without a cornerstone, the foundation would fall apart. To destroy a building constructed in this way, all you have to do is move the cornerstone!

If you are a male, you are God's foundation for your family, but it's an *interlocking* foundation that needs something strong to hold it secure. Jesus Christ Himself is the only hope for your continued survival and effectiveness as the foundation of your family because He is the Chief Cornerstone. *"He only is my rock and my salvation; He is my defense; I shall not be moved"* (Psalm 62:6 NKJV).

⁓

*Thought*: Without the Chief Cornerstone, the family's foundation will fall apart.

*Readings*: Psalm 27:1–5; Ephesians 2:19–20

# —DAY 45—
## ANCHORING THE SHIP

*"We have this hope as an anchor for the soul, firm and secure."* —Hebrews 6:19

Merriam-Webster's 11th Collegiate Dictionary defines *anchor* as "a reliable or principal support: mainstay" and "something that serves to hold an object firmly." Another definition is "anything that gives stability and security." You need stability and security in an environment that is unstable and insecure. This is a description of the world we live in.

Men serve not only as the foundation, but also as the anchor of the human family. As a verb, *anchor* means "to fasten, to stop, or to rest." Men are supposed to "fasten" the society—to secure it with beliefs and principles that don't change. The male is also supposed to stop things from happening that are harmful to others. I am amazed at what men allow to happen—in their homes, with their children, in their communities. As anchors, men can stop their families from being swept away by the currents of immorality, stabilize uncertain youth, and bring safety and order back to communities. An anchor also brings rest: when people have a true anchor present in their lives, they experience an inner peace.

Men, you should think of your family as a ship, and you as the anchor of that ship. A ship has no foundation of its own. The hull, the masts, the sails, the rigging, and even the helm can't fulfill that function. Your boat may look beautiful on the outside; yet, by itself, it contains no foundation. The only thing that secures a boat is an anchor. When the anchor is in place, the entire hull comes to rest. Even if the ship is beaten, twisted, and torn by waves, a strong anchor keeps it from breaking apart and allows it to weather the storms.

～

*Thought*: Men are supposed to "fasten" society—to secure it with beliefs and principles that don't change.

*Readings*: Jeremiah 6:16; Matthew 5:13–16

# AN EQUAL PARTNER

*"The LORD God said, 'It is not good for the man to be alone. I will make a helper suitable for him.'"*     —Genesis 2:18

Genesis tells us that God presented every animal to the man, but none was suitable for him. (See Genesis 2:19–20.) There was no one to whom he could relate, no one who could help him in his proprietorship of the earth. So, God said, in essence, "It's not good for man to be alone in one body." It is impossible for love to love alone. Thus, God created the woman. Remember, the primary purpose of the female was to receive love from the male, just as God's major purpose for creating the spirit-man was to have a relationship of love with mankind.

*"It is not good for the man to be alone. I will make a helper suitable for him."* I don't think that men can read or hear this Scripture often enough. You might not think that a man who has a close relationship with God; who understands his role as foundation; who has been given the vision; and who can lead, teach, cultivate, provide, and protect needs anyone else. Yet even a man who knows and lives in his purpose is not complete, according to God. The male needs a companion, someone to be his helper—not as a subordinate or a sidekick, but as an equal partner with a complementary purpose. This is as true for single men as it is for married men. Men need women as fellow workers and colleagues in this world if they are to fulfill their purpose in life.

In the family, the father is the head as a result of God's timing and creation. Yet, again, this does not mean the woman is inferior to him. The woman was created by God to be a helper, not a slave. There is a big difference between the two. The Bible refers to the

Holy Spirit as a Helper. (See John 15:26; 16:7 NKJV.) Jesus said that the Holy Spirit not only would help us, but also would lead us. *"He will guide you into all truth"* (John 16:13 NKJV, KJV). The Holy Spirit is the *Paraclete*, meaning the One who comes alongside to help, as well as to be a Comforter, Counselor, and Guide.

Being a helper does not mean being inferior. A helper can be a guide and a teacher. Therefore, although the male is always the responsible head in God's design, he is not the "boss." He is not the owner of the woman.

Remember that when God addresses the human race, He never addresses us as male and female; He addresses us as "man." He deals with the spirit-man within both male and female. In order to function on earth as mankind, however, males and females each exercise an aspect of leadership.

While the male is ultimately the responsible head, the female is the coleader. A good illustration of this is the relationship between Jesus and His church. Jesus is called the Head, and the church is called the body. (See Colossians 1:18.) They work in unison with one another. Christ's relationship to the church is the perfect model for us of the male-female relationship and God's purposes for the woman in her dominion leadership role.

*Thought*: Christ's relationship to the church is the perfect model for us of the male-female relationship.

*Readings*: Psalm 133:1; Ephesians 1:22–23

# — DAY 47 —
## DISTINCT, NOT SUPERIOR OR INFERIOR

*"Heirs with you of the gracious gift of life."* —1 Peter 3:7

Today, many of those who advocate equal rights say that there is no difference at all between men and women. Yet we have seen that, while men and women were created equal, they were also created distinct. This is part of their unique design. This statement may confuse some people and anger others, because somehow we have come to believe that *different* means *inferior* or *superior*. Don't confuse being different with being either greater or lesser. Different does not imply superiority or inferiority; different simply means different. This is especially true in regard to men and women; their differences are necessary because of their purposes.

In many spheres of life, we don't consider differences to be weaknesses but rather mutual strengths. In music, who is more important to a full symphony orchestra, a violin player or an oboe player? Both work together in harmony. In sports, who is more important to a swimming medley relay, the swimmer who swims the breaststroke or the swimmer who swims the backstroke? Both have to be strong swimmers in their particular specialties, because a medley race cannot be swum with only one type of swimmer. When they win, they share the honor together.

The answer to the historical devaluing of women does not lie in declaring that there are no differences between females and males, but in recognizing and affirming their complementary differences. We must understand and accept these differences so they can be used in harmony, like a finely tuned orchestra.

God's intent that women be equal heirs with men in creation and redemption remains largely an ignored truth. Men's internal devaluing of women is the reason women generally continue to be discounted and exploited in almost every society in the world, regardless of recent social and political advances. In developed nations as well as developing nations, the plight of the female is still very real. It is tragic to have to admit this is true in our modern society.

Many women are involved in opportunities and activities that were formerly reserved for males, such as leadership, management, and sports. However, although we can say that there has been some improvement, in most societies, women are still suffering the prejudice of the male against the female. Men's hearts cannot be changed by legislation. Even though the law now says, "Women are equal to men," this doesn't mean that men think so. The persistent devaluing of women continues to hold back progress, and women are being treated in every way *except* in the way God originally intended: *"heirs with you of the gracious gift of life."* Through God's grace, we can restore the relationships between women and men and fulfill God's original purposes for mankind.

⤿

*Thought*: God's intent that women be equal heirs with men in creation and redemption remains largely an ignored truth.

*Readings*: Genesis 1:26–28; Ephesians 5:28

# — DAY 48 —
## A MUTUAL SUBMITTING

*"A man ought not to cover his head, since he is the image and glory of God; but the woman is the glory of man."*
—1 Corinthians 11:7

In our opening verse, Paul was saying that once the man is covered with Christ, his marriage is under authority. However, the woman then needs the man to cover her. First Corinthians 11:9–10 says, *"Neither was man created for woman, but woman for man. For this reason, and because of the angels, the woman ought to have a sign of authority on her head"* (NIV84).

If you want to do a work for God, all of heaven is ready to work for you. God says, "All right, we'll do spiritual work, but how are your relationships in the natural realm? What is your relationship with your wife, your family members, the members of your church?" Any man who says, "I don't need the church; I can do this by myself," isn't going to find any angels supporting him. The angels are looking for your authority. They will ask, "Whom are you under? How can you expect us to help you under God's authority when you yourself aren't under anybody?" Submission activates heaven.

Now, if Christ submitted to the Father, who do we think we are? You may be independent, famous, a fantastic businessperson, and doing very well. However, if you aren't going to submit to anyone, heaven won't trust you. Don't believe that you can run off and do God's work without being in submission. Don't ever run away from a ministry and do your own work because somebody there made you upset. The angels are watching. You may actually remove God's protective covering from yourself when you move out from under your authority. This spiritual principle applies to both males and females.

Yet here's what most people forget when it comes to submission: men and women are created to be *inter*dependent. *"In the Lord, however, woman is not independent of man, nor is man independent of woman"* (1 Corinthians 11:11 NIV84). God is saying, in effect, "Men and women need one another. They need each other to be complete."

*"For as woman came from man, so also man is born of woman"* (verse 12). I like that statement. Men need women to give birth to them, but women need men to enable them to conceive. This is definitely not an inferiority-superiority situation. It has to do with complementary purposes. Ephesians 5, which talks about wives submitting to their husbands, also says, ***"Submit to one another out of reverence for Christ"*** (verse 21). There has to be a mutual submitting to one another if God's purposes are to be carried out on the earth.

⌣

*Thought*: If you won't submit to anyone, heaven won't trust you.

*Readings*: Isaiah 66:1–2; Romans 13:1–3

# THE SAME SPIRITUAL POSITION

*"In the Lord woman is not independent of man, nor is man independent of woman. For as woman came from man, so also man is born of woman. But everything comes from God."*
—1 Corinthians 11:11–12

After Paul taught that woman came from man and was created for man, he then placed both male and female in the same spiritual position.

My wife and I are equal before the Lord. She can go before the Lord and get the same spiritual help that I get. She doesn't need to go through me, her husband. *The essence of the matter is this:* in the spiritual realm, there is no difference between men and women, but in the physical realm, there has to be the proper relationship of submission.

Once, I was speaking to a woman who is in management at an insurance company. She told me, "You know, at work, I'm the boss. Yet when I walk through the door into my home, I'm a wife." That's a smart woman. Of course, she can be the boss at work. But when she gets home, she's a wife, and her husband is her head, or authority. That means she can't treat her husband like one of her employees at the office. An altogether different authority takes over. Yet a husband has to understand that he is supposed to be in the Lord when he's in the home, and that he himself is under God's authority.

Similarly, a woman's ultimate Source and Provider is God, and she can always turn to Him. But God has designed things so that the female can receive earthly provision through the male. *"Man did not come from woman, but woman from man"* (1 Corinthians

11:8) means that the man is responsible for the woman because she came from man. This is God's original plan.

Again, if a man starts thinking that this is *his* plan, rather than God's, his responsibility for the woman will turn into domination over her. We have to understand that the female's provision by the male is God's design, or we will misuse and abuse it.

The man is responsible for providing because of his position in the relationship of things. There is a parallel to this in the spiritual realm. Spiritually, we are to go to God for what we need. Jesus has told us, "Remain in Me and I will remain in you. If you are separated from Me, you can't do anything. I am the Vine; you are the branches, which receive nourishment from the Vine." (See John 15:4–5.)

*Thought*: In the spiritual realm, there is no difference between men and women.

*Readings*: Genesis 1:27; John 15:4–5

# — Day 50 —

# RESTORING DAMAGE FROM THE FALL

*"Husbands, love your wives and do not be harsh with them."*
—Colossians 3:19

Why must husbands be *commanded* to love their wives? It is because the fall damaged the male's God-given natural love for the female, so that he wants *to rule over her* rather than *to love her as himself.* This is why, as the male is being restored to God's original design through redemption in Christ, he needs to be instructed to love the woman. For the same reason, the female's God-given natural *respect* for the male was damaged, and that is why she needs to be instructed to respect him. Thus, when God's purposes are restored, peace is reestablished between males and females. However, when the fallen nature is allowed free reign, there is discord.

When Paul said, *"Husbands, love your wives, just as Christ loved the church and gave himself up for her...* (Ephesians 5:25), he was saying, in effect, "Husband, above all else, love your wife. Don't worry about other things before that, because you can take care of those things in due course. If you love her, you will take care of many other problems and potential problems in your marriage. With love, she will function properly, because she was born to be loved."

Remember, a woman will reflect the love that she receives. When she is loved, she is better able to live a life of joy and peace, even in the midst of difficult circumstances. When she is unloved, it is as if there is a weight on her heart. Any man who violates a woman's need for love is misusing and abusing God's purpose for the woman.

"...to make her holy, cleansing her by the washing with water through the word" (Ephesians 5:26). What does it mean for a husband to wash his wife with the Word? Christ is our example in this. Every time we have a negative experience, Jesus comes in immediately with a positive one and washes away the negative. Husbands are to do the same for their wives.

For instance, when the disciples were afraid, Jesus said, "Be of good cheer" (Matthew 14:27 KJV). Every time they became nervous, He told them to remain calm. Whenever they became frightened by a storm, He told them to relax. He was always there to wash away fear, to wash away doubt. When they wondered how they were going to feed the five thousand, He told them to have faith. He was always washing His church with God's truth.

What kind of man do we need today? When your wife says, "We're not going to be able to pay the mortgage," you say, "Honey, we serve the God of Abraham, Isaac, and Jacob, the God of my grandparents and parents. Let's just keep standing on the Word. It's going to be all right." That's washing your wife.

God wants men who will stand up in their faith, saying, "A thousand may fall on my right, and ten thousand on my left, but in this house we're going to come through. My house is covered by the Word of God. As for me and my house, we're going to be all right." That's a man; that's a washer, filled with the Word of God!

*Thought*: God wants men who will stand up in their faith.

*Readings*: Joshua 24:15; John 14:27

# — DAY 51 —
## RESPECTING AND AFFIRMING WOMEN

*"Husbands, in the same way be considerate as you live with your wives, and treat them with respect."* —1 Peter 3:7

Husbands, love your wives, just as Christ also loved the church and gave Himself for her, that He might sanctify...her"* (Ephesians 5:25–26 NKJV). If a man is going to love his wife, he has to keep company with Christ. He has to find out how Christ loved His church. It will take a lifetime to study that manual on love! He *"gave Himself for her."* Then He sanctified her.

To sanctify something means to take it away from all else, set it apart in a special place, care for it every day, and value it as a priceless gem. To sanctify something means that you do not allow anything near it that would hurt or destroy it. It is set apart for special use. This means that you don't pass it around. It is not available to entertain other people.

The man should love the woman because she was drawn from him and is a part of him. If he doesn't love her, it is the equivalent of the man hating himself. (See Ephesians 5:29.) A husband treats himself well when he treats his wife well. The man's role, then, is to love his wife as himself, with all the attributes of love that are found in 1 Corinthians 13. When you give a woman love, she comes alive. Yet when she receives anything less than genuine love, it is as if she short-circuits. When you don't love a woman, you are abusing her very nature.

When a man really loves his wife, he considers her the crème de la crème. When she receives such love, she will reflect it in her countenance, the way she looks at life, and in her interactions with others.

These principles of a woman's need to receive love have mainly been expressed in the setting of the marriage relationship. However, they can be more broadly applied. Just as women can be a spiritual help and encouragement not only to their husbands but also to other men they encounter in their lives, men can do the same for women. They can help build a woman's self-esteem by valuing her and treating her with kindness and Christian love. Women need the affirmation of men, just as men need the respect of women. This is particularly important for men to understand, since they are often in positions in authority over women—in the church, in the workplace, and in other realms of life—and they influence their perspectives and attitudes. Of course, this affirmation must always be given with wisdom, so that women never get the idea that the man is expressing anything more than a Christlike concern.

Again, we can turn to 1 Corinthians 13 as the man's guide to respecting and affirming women in any interaction or relationship he has with them. Men need to remember that females who are under their authority or supervision need to be treated with consideration so that the nature that God has given them will not be quenched. Women often reflect the manner in which they are treated by men; if men reflect the love and nature of Christ in their dealings with women, the women also can reflect the love and nature of Christ.

⌒

*Thought*: Women often reflect the manner in which they are treated by men.

*Readings*: Psalm 86:15; 1 Corinthians 13

# — Day 52 —
## NURTURE HER POTENTIAL

*"Therefore encourage one another and build each other up."*
—1 Thessalonians 5:11

While men have a special responsibility for cultivating their wives, they often have unrealistic ideas about women, so they can end up neglecting or hurting them. Most of us men are walking around with specific pictures in our minds of who we want our wives to be, and, when they don't meet our expectations, we tend to blame them. At one point, God showed me that I had this attitude toward my wife, and He had to correct me.

Here's the way a man often thinks: he is a certain type of man, so he wants a certain type of woman. He has ideas such as these: "I am a musician, so I want her to sing." "I'm a banker, so I want her to know about finance." "I am slim, so I want her to be slim." "I want her to be smart." "I want a woman who dresses well." "I like long hair on a woman." Now, there isn't anything wrong with desiring these things. However, I want to tell you something: *the "perfect" woman you are looking for does not exist.*

It is your job to cultivate your wife so that she can be all that *God* created her to be. You are to help her to blossom and grow into God's woman, not tear her down because she doesn't meet your specifications. In addition, you can help your wife become all that you saw in her when you first met her, and which you now think is missing. You need to nurture all the potential she has. This is not to be done in a controlling way, but in a loving and giving way, which is the nature of Christ. Think about it: what pressures are present in her life that are keeping her from being all that she desires and needs to be?

*Thought*: It is your job to cultivate your wife so that she can be all that God created her to be.

*Readings*: Proverbs 12:25; Hebrews 10:24–25

# — DAY 53 —

## PARENTS AND PURPOSE

*"Fathers, do not exasperate your children; instead, bring them up in the training and instruction of the Lord."*
—Ephesians 6:4

Did Jesus have an adolescent problem? The answer is, very simply, no. Why? One reason is that His purpose was reinforced by His earthly father and mother from birth. Somehow, I believe that God would love for all parents to know Him so well that they would have an idea of the life purpose of their children.

The angel Gabriel said to Mary, *"You will conceive and give birth to a son, and you are to call him Jesus. He will be great and will be called the Son of the Most High"* (Luke 1:31–32). An angel of the Lord told Joseph, *"You are to give him the name Jesus, because he will save his people from their sins"* (Matthew 1:21). When Jesus was born, Mary and Joseph could talk to Him about His purpose. Even though, at the time, they didn't fully understand the implications of His name, they could tell Him, "You're going to be a Savior." The Hebrew meaning of the name *Jesus* is "Jehovah-saved," or "the Lord is salvation." In essence, Jesus's name means "Savior."

I can't emphasize strongly enough that knowing your purpose is crucial for your life's course. Every young person comes to a time when he or she leaves childhood and enters adulthood. This is the time when they are trying to discover who they are and why they are. This is also often the time when we lose them or gain them— lose them to a destructive lifestyle and a wasted life or gain them for a positive, fulfilling future. Purpose, therefore, is a key to a young person's effectiveness and happiness in life.

Proverbs 19:18 says, *"Discipline your children, for in that there is hope; do not be a willing party to their death."* This is serious business. The verse is saying, "Discipline and train a child now because there is hope in that discipline, hope in that training." You are giving hope to your child when you discipline and correct them because *you are giving them a value system for their entire life!*

The above verse makes the strong statement that if you don't do this, you may be a party to your child's death. Proverbs 29:15 says, *"A child left undisciplined disgraces its mother."* Check out the children in the reform schools. Check out the inmates in the prisons. Observe the young people who have little sense of direction or morality. Many of them were left to themselves as children, with no one to teach them character and values.

*Thought*: When you discipline and correct your child, you are giving them a value system for their entire life.

*Readings*: Proverbs 1:1–9; Luke 2

## "DAD IS DESTINY"

*"When the foundations are being destroyed, what can the righteous do?"* —Psalm 11:3

Dad is destiny." The words sprang from the page in *U.S. News & World Report*[1] and exploded in my mind like an atom bomb. I could not believe what I was reading. Even more surprising was the source from which I was reading those words—words that seemed to spring from the heart of one of my seminars.

For thirty years, I have lectured and counseled thousands of individuals on the subjects of relationships, family development, and marriage. One of the greatest concerns I have carried over these years is the male crisis facing most of our communities. I emphatically believe that the key to the restoration and preservation of a sane and healthy society is the salvaging of the male, especially as a responsible father. Reading those words in such a popular news magazine gave me great encouragement.

It is a source of enormous comfort and relief to see that contemporary behavioral scientists, psychologists, and government bodies are finally agreeing with what Christian leaders have known all along.

The statement "Dad is destiny" embodies both the problem and the solution for the majority of society's ills. In it lies the key to the salvation and restoration of mankind. About twenty-five hundred years ago, the prophet Malachi spoke of the work and purpose of the coming Messiah, declaring, *"He will turn the hearts of the fathers to their children, and the hearts of the children to their*

---

1. Joseph P. Shapiro, Joannie M. Schrof, Mike Tharp, and Dorian Friedman, "Honor Thy Children," *U.S. News & World Report*, February 27, 1995.

*fathers*" (Malachi 4:6 niv84). In this Scripture we see the divine assessment of man's fundamental problem—a fatherless society!

The church cannot fix society's problems when the foundation is out of place. As we read in the Psalms, *"When the foundations are being destroyed, what can the righteous do?"* (Psalm 11:3). No matter how much the church works at correcting social ills, if the foundation that God laid for the family is not in place, even the work of the righteous will not be successful. The devil does not care as much if the church is filled with women, because as long as men do not come back to their heavenly Father, then the women and their children are fatherless. Fatherhood is the foundation of the family, the church, and the culture.

If societies and nations have problems with drugs, unwed mothers, corruption, and violence, then they must go back to the foundation in order to solve these problems. If they have a national problem, then they must go back into the communities to find the problem. Community problems are rooted in the families that make up each community. When we check to see what the families' problems are, we must look at marriages. When we examine the condition of our marriages, we discover that husbands and wives are divorced, mothers have been abandoned, and men are not sustaining their families.

What does all this boil down to? Brothers, we are at the root of the problem affecting the nations! The foundational source has a problem: men are not being the fathers God created them to be.

*Thought*: The statement "Dad is destiny" embodies both the problem and the solution for the majority of society's ills.

*Readings*: Malachi 4:1–6; Titus 2:1–8

— DAY 55 —

# KNOW YOUR HEAVENLY FATHER

*Jesus answered and said to him, "If anyone loves Me, he will keep My word; and My Father will love him, and We will come to him and make Our home with him."*

—John 14:23 (NKJV)

After Jesus rose from the dead, He made the wonderful statement, *"I am returning to my Father and your Father, to my God and your God"* (John 20:17 NIV84). Because of Jesus's death and resurrection on our behalf, we can know God not only as our Creator, but also as our Father.

A man won't be able to understand what it means to be a good father if he doesn't know his heavenly Father. A man must also have faith in God as his Father—that He will love, protect, and provide for him. Trust and reliance on God is what a father needs to model for his children. They must see a strong walk of faith in their father's life, both when things are going well and when life is beset with difficulties. The greatest heritage a man can leave his sons and daughters is not money or property but faith. When your child grows up, their house might burn down or be repossessed, but no one can destroy the faith you have instilled in them. Besides, the child will be able to use their faith to obtain another house, because they have been taught to trust God as their Provider.

In the Bible, you will often see variations on the phrase "the God of my father." (See, for example, Genesis 26:24; 32:9; 2 Chronicles 17:4; Isaiah 38:5.) If your children have seen God reflected in you, then you have displayed His life and character to them. In doing so, you have given them a true spiritual heritage.

*"I write to you, fathers, because you have known him who is from the beginning"* (1 John 2:13 NIV84).

In Deuteronomy 4:9, God is saying to men, "Don't let My ways out of your sight. Make sure you understand and obey them first." Then, *"teach them to your children and to their children after them."* Why? Because you are supposed to be the teacher.

Don't just tell your children, "Do this" or "Don't do that." Show them. Watch your life and make sure you keep the Word of God. Some men say one thing but do another. For example, they may tell their children to be honest but then call off work when they're not sick. Some fathers tell their children, "Tobacco is bad for you"; meanwhile, they're puffing away on a cigarette. Children see this and think, "To be a grown-up, you have to smoke." Adults reinforce this idea by their actions. God tells us not to do this to our children. People don't seem to understand that you cannot teach something if you're not being a model of it yourself.

Where, again, does the father get his original instruction and information so he can teach it? From God the Father and His Word. As we have seen, even if a father has not been fathered by a godly man, he can return to our heavenly Father and learn God's ways. He can receive godly instruction from his pastor and righteous men in the church who know and love the Word of God. And, of course, a father who is a born-again believer has the Holy Spirit within him, teaching him everything that the Son hears from the Father. (See John 16:5–15.)

⌒

*Thought*: The greatest heritage a man can leave his sons and daughters is not money or property but faith.

*Readings*: Deuteronomy 4:1–14; John 14:19–23

# —DAY 56—
## BE RESPONSIBLE FOR YOUR CHILDREN

*"Our fathers disciplined us for a little while as they thought best; but God disciplines us for our good, that we may share in his holiness."* —Hebrews 12:10 (NIV84)

Many fathers don't really want to take responsibility for their children, because children take time and energy. Therefore, they leave them to fend for themselves. Balancing all of life's demands can be difficult for a father, but your children should be at the top of the list, after your wife.

How much time do you spend with your children? Who is really bringing them up? Perhaps you and your wife leave for work early in the morning and don't return until late in the evening. Someone else has brought them up all day. Realize that everything that person represents goes into your children. They will learn their views of God, their concept of themselves, and their philosophy of life from their caretaker.

A father's responsibility also includes disciplining his children, but some men don't have the backbone for it. They are afraid to correct their children, so they leave it up to their wives. The Bible doesn't tell the mother to correct the children; it says the father is to discipline them. Yet how many fathers leave discipline up to the mothers? Some fathers don't correct their children because they want the children to like them. They don't realize the effect this has on their families. Their children think, "Daddy doesn't really love me." They may also grow up believing a parent isn't supposed to discipline his children, so they don't become good agents of correction for their own children. There are times when love has to be tough.

Love means correcting, chastening, and reproving your children when they need it. Some children are begging to be corrected, but their fathers don't have any sense to realize it. Some children hate their fathers because they let them do whatever they want. The fathers imagine the children will do fine on their own. They think, "My children are old enough to handle it," while their children are thinking, "I need help, Daddy! I don't know the right values in life. I don't have standards to judge by. I'm looking to you to give me some guidelines, and you're telling me, 'Decide for yourself.'"

Some parents confuse warning with threatening: "I'm going to kill you if you don't stop that!" They don't have any kind of tact because they don't know any better. A child interprets a warning as love but sees a threat as hate.

Loving your children means setting standards for them. Life today is very complex and confusing. Children need someone who can tell them, "This is the way in which to go." You need to give your children a love that instills eternal values. I've talked to parents who were concerned because their child was wayward. "We don't know what happened. We gave him everything he wanted," they said. That was the problem. You don't give your children everything they want. You give them what they need—unconditional love, godly discipline, and eternal values to live by.

Love is not buying gifts. Love is *you being a gift.* The Bible tells us that our heavenly Father so loved the world that He became a revelation of that love in Jesus Christ. Therefore, if a man is really a father, he doesn't just send gifts. He sends himself. That's the essence of love.

*Thought*: Who is really raising your children?

*Readings*: Proverbs 3:11–12; Romans 14:11–12

# — DAY 57 —
## TEACH YOUR CHILDREN AND GRANDCHILDREN

*"Teach them to your children and to their children after them."* —Deuteronomy 4:9

In Deuteronomy 4, Moses gave instructions from God to the heads of households about teaching their families God's ways:

> *Be careful, and watch yourselves closely so that you do not forget the things your eyes have seen or let them fade from your heart as long as you live. Teach them to your children and to their children after them.* (Deuteronomy 4:9)

God is very concerned that parents teach their children about Him. He isn't saying here to send your children to church, Sunday school, or vacation Bible club. He's saying to teach them yourself. These other activities are good, but if what they teach is not reinforced in the home, children can get the impression their parents don't think the Bible is important. Parents don't realize the negative impact this attitude can have on their families.

*"...and to their children after them."* I want to say a word here to grandparents. When your daughter or son sends that little boy or girl to you, what does the child go back home with? Some kids learn things from their grandparents that are disgraceful. Parents find their little children coming back home cursing or telling foul stories, and they wonder where they are hearing these things. They're getting them from Grandpa and Grandma! Your children's children should get the Word from you. Timothy received a strong spiritual heritage from both his mother and his grandmother. Paul wrote, *"I am reminded of your sincere faith, which first lived in your*

*grandmother Lois and in your mother Eunice and, I am persuaded, now lives in you also"* (2 Timothy 1:5).

Fathers and grandfathers should also pass along a strong spiritual heritage to their descendants. When your children send their kids to you, those kids should go back home knowing more about God.

⌒

*Thought:* God is very concerned that parents teach their children about Him.

*Readings:* Proverbs 20:15; Ephesians 4:29

# —DAY 58—
## FORTIFY YOUR CHILDREN
## THROUGH THE WORD

*"These commandments that I give you today are to be upon your hearts. Impress them on your children. Talk about them when you sit at home and when you walk along the road, when you lie down and when you get up. Tie them as symbols on your hands and bind them on your foreheads. Write them on the doorframes of your houses and on your gates."*
—Deuteronomy 6:6–9 (NIV84)

Reflecting on the above Scripture passage, let's look at four specific ways in which God told Moses that parents are to talk to their children about His commandments.

*"Talk about them when you sit at home."* What do your children hear in your house? What do they hear when you sit down to eat? Some scandal reported in the newspaper? The latest movie? What do you discuss? Do you talk about the goodness of the Lord? When you sit around your house during your leisure time, what do you do? Do you spend time teaching your children the Word? Do you have family devotions?

*"Talk about them…when you walk along the road."* What do you talk about when you drive your children to school or go on trips? Do you yell at other drivers or listen to less-than-edifying radio shows? What example do you set for your children when you're out in public? Do you talk about others behind their backs? Or do you live out God's Word in a natural, everyday way?

*"Talk about them…when you lie down"* (Deuteronomy 6:7). Before you say good night to your children or tuck them into bed, what words do you leave them with? The assurance of God's

presence and peace during the night? An encouraging psalm? Or do you wave them off to bed while you finish working on something?

In fact, what do *you* think about before you drift off to sleep? Do you know that the last thing you think about at night is usually the first thing you think about when you wake up? Sometimes you dream about it. It amazes me that people deliberately think about the worst things. You may be reading the worst kind of books before you go to bed. Then you wonder why your spirit is disturbed.

*"Talk about them...when you get up."* When you wake up in the morning, you will more likely think about the Word of God if you have meditated on it before going to bed. And you will start ministering as you talk about it with your family.

How do you usually greet your children in the morning? With a quiet reminder of God's love and strength for the day? With what spiritual armor do you send them off to school? It's a difficult world for children to grow up in today, and they need God's Word to fortify them for daily living.

⌒

*Thought*: Children need the Word of God to fortify them for daily living.

*Readings*: Deuteronomy 6; James 1:22–25

# —Day 59—
## CONDITION YOUR CHILDREN

*"Train a child in the way he should go, and when he is old he will not turn from it."* —Proverbs 22:6 (NIV84)

If you train your children, they will grow up to know God's ways and to have peace in their hearts. The things children learn from their parents never leave them. I still retain what my father and mother taught me. The same temptations that come to any young man came to me. What kept me on an even keel were the values and morals that were instilled in me. There were situations where, if it wasn't for the training of my parents, I would have gone under. What kept me safe was the character I learned from their teaching and correction. I love my parents because they disciplined me.

My parents had a wonderful way of sitting me down and saying, "Now, here is why we disciplined you." They didn't just punish me; they corrected me. They said, "If you keep this up, this will happen," and "If you keep this kind of company, this will be the result." Disciplining your children will be painful for both you and your children at times, but the results will be positive and healthy.

My heart goes out to single parents who have to fill the roles of both father and mother. I strongly want to encourage you not to let your children train you. Don't allow them to reverse the roles of parent and child. You may not know everything in life, but you know more than they do! And that's enough for you to be in charge. I don't care how old they are, when you're paying the mortgage, when you're providing for them, you make the rules. If they disobey the rules, you have to make sure they experience the consequences.

*"Train a child in the way he should go..."* (Proverbs 22:6 NIV84). The word for *"train"* in this verse is the same word that is used for conditioning. The Bible is saying, "Condition your child in the way he should go." Why? He can't condition himself. He was born with a rebellious spirit. You don't have to teach your children to swear, lie, steal, commit adultery, or have bitterness and hatred. It's already in them. If you don't condition them, they will naturally become wayward. You have to train them. If you seek and trust Him, the Lord will provide everything you need to help you fulfill this role, whether you are part of a two-parent family or are a single parent.

⌐⌐⌐

*Thought*: Disciplining your children will be painful for both you and your children at times, but the results will be positive and healthy.

*Readings*: Proverbs 29:17; Ephesians 6:1–4

# —DAY 60—
## ENCOURAGE AND COMFORT YOUR CHILDREN

*"For you know that we dealt with each of you as a father deals with his own children, encouraging, comforting and urging* [or warning] *you to live lives worthy of God, who calls you into his kingdom and glory."*     —1 Thessalonians 2:11–12

Children need encouragement. Some children never hear an encouraging word from their parents. Do you hear how some parents talk to their children? They act as if the children can't do anything right. They don't remember what it is like to be a child, and they expect their children to have adult skills. A ten-year-old boy is washing the dishes. His father comes in and says, "Can't you clean dishes better than this?" The little guy is at least trying. So encourage him. Maybe he leaves a little soap on the stove or counter. Don't look at what he left; look at what he cleaned up. Encourage him.

Maybe your child can't read quite as fast as you did when you were her age. Don't criticize her. Encourage her. Some children are really trying. Sometimes a child will try to help out with the chores and will unintentionally break something. His mother will run into the room and yell, "What are you doing?" He gets a lecture. So he goes to his room with a broken heart, a depressed spirit, and a hurt ego. He thinks, "I'm not going to help ever again!" Some parents don't see their child's intention. They see only their own anger and frustration. So, correct and instruct your children with patience, and encourage their efforts.

Children also need comforting. You encourage them when they're doing something positive and when you want them to improve in something. But there will be times when they become discouraged, hurt, confused, or disillusioned. That is when they need comfort.

How can you comfort your children? By letting them know they are loved, even when they make mistakes or don't live up to your expectations. By listening to their struggles and problems with kindness and understanding. By giving them warm embraces and loving words when they are sad. By remembering the times God has comforted you in your distress and giving that same comfort to them.

To be a comforter, you have to be accessible to your children. You have to know what's going on in their lives so you can know when they're experiencing struggles and loneliness. Children will be comforted to know you're available to them and that you make it a point to spend time with them. Your comfort will also help them to know that their heavenly Father is a Comforter, just as He is described in His Word: *"the Father of compassion and the God of all comfort, who comforts us in all our troubles"* (2 Corinthians 1:3–4).

*Thought*: Comforting your children will help them to know that their heavenly Father is a Comforter.

*Readings*: Job 16:1–5; 2 Corinthians 1:3–6

# —Day 61—
## AN ANCHOR STOPS THINGS

*"Then we will no longer be infants, tossed back and forth by the waves, and blown here and there by every wind of teaching and by the cunning and craftiness of people in their deceitful scheming."* —Ephesians 4:14

Men are called to protect their families and communities from the destructive currents of our modern society. Remember the definitions of an anchor? It is "a reliable or principal support: mainstay," "something that serves to hold an object firmly," and "anything that gives stability and security."

If a boat is drifting with a current, and you put the anchor down on a rock, it stops the boat from being controlled by the current. The current of our modern society is filled with so many strong, ungodly influences that the male needs to come back in the family, put his anchor on the rock of a solid, godly principle, and say, "We're not going in that direction."

Note that an anchor does not stop the current itself. The current will come, but the anchor stops the boat you are in. How many things have you stopped from happening to your son or your daughter? You see your daughter wearing certain clothes or looking a certain way, or you see your son watching something inappropriate on the Internet, and you say, "No, not in this house."

A male is an anchor, and an anchor *stops* things. You may know that your daughter and son are being taught in school that homosexuality is acceptable. As a kingdom father, you have to put the anchor down and say, "That's not from God." Many times, I had to tell my son and daughter, "That music—not in this house. That type of clothing—not in this house. This boat is anchored."

They made it through the turbulent waves of those teen years. My children are upstanding young adults who don't have memories they can't enjoy.

An anchor stops things.

*Thought*: Men are called to protect their families and communities from the destructive currents of our modern society.

*Readings*: Psalm 78:1–8; Ephesians 4:11–15

# PERFECTLY COMPLEMENTARY DESIGNS

*"The eye cannot say to the hand, 'I don't need you!' And the head cannot say to the feet, 'I don't need you!'"*
—1 Corinthians 12:21

God created men and women with perfectly complementary designs. The male is perfect for the female, and the female is perfect for the male. It is when men and women expect each other to think, react, and behave in the same ways—that is, when they don't know or appreciate their God-given differences—that they experience conflict. Yet when they understand and value each other's purposes, they can have rewarding relationships, and they can blend their unique designs harmoniously for God's glory.

Many husbands and wives don't realize that the needs of their spouses are different from their own. There is a principle that "purpose determines nature, and nature determines needs." If a woman wants to help a man fulfill his purpose, she must learn his nature, how he functions, and what his needs are. She can't give him what she needs, because his needs are often different from hers. The reverse is also true. A man must learn a woman's needs and seek to meet them.

God has given strengths to the female that the male does not possess, and vice versa. Until they recognize the natures God has placed within each of them, they will be weak in certain areas, because each was designed to supply what the other lacks. Again, males and females have different strengths, and neither can fully function without the other.

The designs of males and females govern the needs of each that must be met for them to be fulfilled, contented, and living in

God's creation purposes. The problem is that many people are not fully aware of their own needs, let alone the needs of others. Even when people are aware of their needs, they often live in frustration because their needs are not being met. They end up demanding that another person satisfy them or they suffer in silence, never expecting to live a completely fulfilled life.

In the next few days, we will explore the paramount needs of the male and the female that contribute to a fulfilling relationship. Please keep in mind that the needs that are listed as male needs and the needs that are listed as female needs are also the needs of both. However, they will be discussed in the context of the *primary* needs of each.

As we come to understand one another's needs and work to fulfill them, our hearts and minds will be renewed and more of God's creation purposes will be restored to our lives. In this endeavor, Jesus's great principle *"It is more blessed to give than to receive"* (Acts 20:35) is vital. As you give, meeting the needs of others, you will be blessed, and many of your own needs will be met in return.

<hr>

*Thought*: The designs of males and females govern the needs of each that must be met for them to be fulfilled, contented, and living in God's creation purposes.

*Readings*: Genesis 2:23; 1 Corinthians 12:12–26

# —Day 63—
## NEED FOR RESPECT/LOVE

*"Each one of you* [husbands] *also must love his wife as he loves himself, and the wife must respect her husband."*
—Ephesians 5:33

In the above verse, the apostle Paul emphasized the primary needs of men and women, which we began to look at earlier.

Being respected is at the core of a man's self-esteem, and it affects every other area of his life. It is part of his nature as leader, protector, and provider. A wife can meet her husband's need for admiration and respect by understanding his value and achievements more than anyone else. She needs to remind him of his capabilities and help him to maintain his self-confidence. She should be proud of her husband, not out of duty, but as an expression of sincere admiration for the man with whom she has chosen to share her life.

We should remember that a single man needs respect as much as a married man does. He needs the respect and affirmation of women because he is designed to need it. The women in a single man's life can meet his need by recognizing his value and accomplishments as a man and by encouraging him in his talents and lifework.

As much as a man needs to know that he is respected, a woman needs to feel that she is loved. Because she was created for the purpose of receiving love, a woman doesn't just desire love; she truly requires it. A woman wants to feel that she is important and special to her husband. When a man spends time with a woman, it makes her feel cherished because she knows she comes first in his life. She feels cared for when he goes out of his way to make sure she has everything she needs.

Because the female's primary need is for love, she often thinks that the male's primary need is for love, also. He needs love, but his need for respect is even greater. If a female expresses love to a male without fulfilling his need for respect, he might not respond in the way she expects him to. He might remain somewhat distant. For example, a woman may wonder why her husband doesn't seem satisfied in the relationship when she has been lovingly trying to help him by keeping the household running smoothly and providing for his material needs. A woman might even write her husband love notes and give him lots of affection but notice that he still doesn't seem happy. She wonders, "What else can I do for this man?"

Yet a male feels about those things in the same way that a female feels about the male's provision of a house. He is grateful that his material and emotional needs are being taken care of, and he appreciates his wife's efforts. However, these things don't address his primary need. A husband is to love and cherish his wife. A wife is to respect and honor her husband. In this way, there will be a constant meeting of the other's primary needs.

◟⁓⁓⁓⁓⁓⁓◞

*Thought*: Build up your spouse by meeting her primary need.

*Readings*: Proverbs 31:23; 1 Peter 1:22

# — DAY 64 —
## NEED FOR RECREATION/CONVERSATION

*"The pleasantness of a friend springs from their heartfelt
advice."*                                              —Proverbs 27:9

A man's competitive nature leads to his need for recreational
companionship, his need to be involved in challenging activities.
Although he likes to win, he also desires to share these experiences
with others. Nothing blesses a man more than when a woman is
involved in his favorite recreation. If a wife participates in what
her husband enjoys doing and lets him tell her all about it, she can
strengthen her relationship with him. He will feel good that she is
involved in his interests.

I've heard women say things like this about their husbands:
"That old fool; he's always over at the ball field playing softball.
I wish he would stop that and come home and be a husband."
This attitude won't help the situation. He has a need that is being
met out there on the ball field. Why would a man spend hours
on something unless he has a need that is being fulfilled through
it? Instead of fighting against what brings fulfillment to the man,
the woman should find out why it is important to him. Then, if
possible, she should participate in it so that they can experience it
together, thus building understanding, companionship, and intimacy in their relationship.

A woman has a need for conversation. Yet, because males have
a leadership mindset, sometimes their conversations with their
wives amount to instructions rather than a give-and-take dialogue.
A woman desires to have a man talk *with* her, not *at* her.

Some men don't realize that a woman has a need to express
herself and therefore has much within her that she wants to share.

A man can fulfill a woman's need for intimate conversation by continually making a point to communicate with her. To truly meet her need, he should talk with her at the *feeling* level and not just the knowledge and information level. She needs him to listen to her attitudes about the events of her day with sensitivity, interest, and concern, resisting the impulse to offer quick solutions. Instead, he should offer his full attention and understanding. All of his conversations with her should convey a desire to understand her, not to change her.

*Thought*: A male needs to share his interests, and a female needs conversation: these related needs can be a wonderful bridge of communication between men and women.

*Readings*: Genesis 2:18; John 4:4–39

# — DAY 65 —
## NEED FOR SEX/AFFECTION

*"My beloved is mine and I am his."*   —Song of Songs 2:16

One of the male's primary needs is sex, while one of the female's primary needs is affection. If these two interrelated needs are not lovingly understood and balanced, they can cause some of the worst conflicts in a marriage.

The man is the provider of the seed, and therefore his natural inclination is to provide this source. This is one of the reasons why he concentrates on the event of sex. The woman, on the other hand, is the one who gestates the new life. Her role is to provide a warm and secure environment in which the life can grow and develop. As an incubator, the woman's natural focus is on the sensory, intuitive, and emotional realms of life, and this is why she has a corresponding need for affection. She needs an environment of affection in order to feel loved and fulfilled.

It is important for a woman to be sensitive to her husband's need for sex. Sometimes a woman sees a man's sexual energy as animalistic and thoughtless. If his approach is too abrupt or too aggressive, she may tell him to leave her alone. There are also times when she is not ready for sexual relations because of her cycle, so she will put him off. In these situations, the man may interpret her refusals as disinterest or disrespect, instead of recognizing the underlying reasons behind them.

A woman doesn't just want affection—she needs it! The problem is that most males are not naturally affectionate. Many men simply do not understand how to give affection to their wives. If a husband is not sure how to be affectionate, he should sit down with his wife and ask her—gently and sincerely.

Giving affection to a woman means appealing to that which makes her an emotional being. Sometimes a woman just wants her husband to sit with her, hold her hand, and talk with her. Her need can also be met by plenty of hugs and kisses; a steady flow of words, cards, and flowers; common courtesies; and meaningful gifts that show that the man is thinking of her—that he esteems her and values her presence in his life.

What women and men need to understand is that *affection creates the environment for sexual union* in marriage, while *sex is the event*. Most men don't realize this, and so they immediately go after the event. They don't know what it means to create an environment of affection. They focus only on their need. Women need affection to precede sexual intimacy.

The Bible says that husbands and wives are to fulfill one another's sexual needs. (See 1 Corinthians 7:3–5.) It also says that a husband is to be sensitive to his wife's overall needs, treating her with kindness and respect. Men and women must balance having their own needs fulfilled with showing consideration for one another.

⌒

*Thought*: Affection creates the environment for sexual union in marriage, while sex is the event.

*Readings*: Genesis 24; 1 Corinthians 7:3–5

# — DAY 66 —
## LOVE EXPRESSED THROUGH AFFECTION

*"My dove in the clefts of the rock, in the hiding places on the mountainside, show me your face, let me hear your voice; for your voice is sweet, and your face is lovely."*
—Song of Songs 2:14

What is affection? One definition is "tender attachment." Women need to have love continually expressed to them through affection, including tender words and gestures.

Men are basically logical and unemotional in their outlook on life, and they have a tendency to treat women in the same manner. Yet because of the way women are designed, they interpret a man's logical approach as coldness. Men need to learn how to love their wives in such a way that they can understand and receive their love. It isn't enough for a man to *think* that he is giving a woman love; he needs to learn the ways in which she receives love. He needs to learn how women in general recognize love, and he needs to learn how his wife *in particular* recognizes love.

Again, a woman functions on love; she needs to hear it expressed often. Many women say that receiving gestures of kindness and tenderness on a regular basis from their husbands, such as physical affection, notes, and flowers, is what communicates love to them. It is not the expense of the gifts as much as the true thoughtfulness behind them and the consistency of receiving them that makes the difference.

Many men believe that they are expressing proper love to their wives by providing them with the essentials in life, such as shelter, food, and clothing, or by giving them expensive items, such as major appliances, cars, and even diamond jewelry. Certainly, many men give these things out of a motivation of love; however, giving such material items is not the essence of love. As we have seen, the essence of love is the giving of oneself. (See Ephesians 5:25.)

*Thought*: Women need to have love expressed to them through affection, including tender words and gestures.

*Readings*: Song of Songs 2:10–13; Ephesians 5:1–2

# SEX IS GOD'S IDEA

*"God saw all that he had made, and it was very good."*
—Genesis 1:31

How do we know that sex is a good thing? God created man and woman and their sexual nature. Therefore, He said that sex is *"very good."*

Unfortunately, sexuality is often extremely misunderstood—not only in the secular world, but also in the church. I am deeply concerned about the damage this lack of understanding about sex has done—and is doing—to people's lives. It has led to confusion and broken relationships between men and women. It has prevented males from living up to their full potential as men and husbands. It has destroyed marriages—and lives. My prayer is that men and women will find wholeness in God as they understand His purpose and plan for human sexuality.

God is not negative about sex. Again, He *created* it. (See Genesis 1:28.) Sex is God's idea, not man's idea. It is such a beautiful expression of love and giving that only God could have thought of it. Men and women were designed as sexual beings. Every baby is born as a sexual creature with the potential to have a sexual relationship as an adult. God is negative only about the *misuse* of sex because it harms the people He created to have a fulfilling relationship with the opposite sex. We must realize that the Bible itself is very open about the subject of sexuality. The main theme of the book of Song of Songs is sexual love. It is the story of a young bridegroom and his bride and their love and desire for one another.

Why did God create sex? The primary reason is that unity is a central aspect of God's nature and purposes. In the Bible, the sexual union of marriage is used as a metaphor to describe the intimacy between Christ and the church. The picture of Christ as the Bridegroom and the church as the bride gives us an idea of the preciousness with which God views sex. He views it as a symbol of His oneness with His beloved humanity, who have been created in His image and redeemed through His love.

*Thought*: God is negative only about the *misuse* of sex because it harms the people He created to have a fulfilling relationship with the opposite sex.

*Readings*: Isaiah 62:4–5; Revelation 19:6–9

# IGNORANCE ABOUT SEXUALITY

*"Do not conform to the pattern of this world, but be transformed by the renewing of your mind."* —Romans 12:2

Some of you are suffering right now from the consequences of uninformed or unwise sexual activity. How a person first learned about sex determines, to a great degree, how he engages in it.

How did you first learn about sexuality? When I've asked men in my seminars how they were introduced to the concept of sex, they've listed various sources, such as friends or peers, movies and television, biology books, pornographic magazines or videos, and sexual experimentation during youth. When we receive our information about sex from one or more of these sources and then pass along this information to others, we perpetuate cultural ignorance about sexuality. This is what has been happening in many of our societies. A lot of what we have learned about sex has been acquired in an unwholesome context, and it is filled with misinformation. Men and women lack positive, informed teaching on the subject of sexuality.

Much of the blame for this lack of teaching falls on the church and the home. In general, the message we've heard from our churches and families is that sex is unholy or dirty and should not be discussed. Young people get the idea that parents and children aren't supposed to talk about sex, because their own parents don't discuss it with them. They are prevented from expressing their sexual questions in the context of a loving home or church community, so they seek information from other sources. When we neglect to teach our children God's truth about sex, then we abandon them to the culture for their information.

No one has a right to shape your child's concept and attitudes about sex, except you. Make sure that a questionable sex education class or *Playboy* magazine isn't your child's teacher. Train your child in the way he or she should go. Then, when a friend or teacher starts to say something erroneous about sex, your child can dismiss it with the knowledge, "That isn't what my parents told me. I know that isn't the truth."

*Thought*: When we neglect to teach our children God's truth about sex, then we abandon them to the culture for their information.

*Readings*: Proverbs 5:15–23; Hebrews 13:4

# A PROTECTIVE BOUNDARY

*"A man leaves his father and mother and is united to his wife, and they become one flesh."* —Genesis 2:24

The boundary God has given us to enjoy sex safely is the marriage covenant. Sex must be engaged in only in the context of marriage—a solemn, lifelong commitment between two people before God.

The Scripture says that a man is to *"bring happiness to the wife he has married"* (Deuteronomy 24:5). It doesn't say to move in with somebody for a year and try things out. There are no provisionary covenants. Solomon said, *"May you rejoice in the wife of your youth.... May her breasts satisfy you always, may you ever be intoxicated with her love"* (Proverbs 5:18–19). This passage is a reference to sex. Enjoy *"the wife of your youth"*—not someone else. There is a vacuum in the male that needs to be filled by the female. And God says, "Make sure your wife is the one who fills that vacuum."

The Scripture says, *"That is why a man leaves his father and mother and is united to his wife, and they become one flesh"* (Genesis 2:24). *"That is why."* For what reason should a man leave? To be *"united."* To whom? *"To his wife."* The minute that law is violated, we begin to reap the repercussions. Verse 24 says, *"And they become one flesh."* The boundary that God has established for the one-flesh experience is the husband-and-wife relationship.

*"All other sins a person commits are outside the body, but whoever sins sexually, sins against their own body"* (1 Corinthians 6:18). Some people can't understand why couples who sleep together and then break off their relationship have trouble going their separate ways. It is because the separation causes real trauma in their souls. This

is a serious matter. That's why relationships outside God's plan can be so dangerous.

Your body belongs to God twice. He didn't just create you; He also redeemed you, and the price was high—the life of His Son Jesus. How can you honor God with your body? First, by waiting until you're married to engage in sex; second, by having sex only with your spouse. You are God's temple. You lift up your hands to worship God; you can use those same hands to caress your spouse. Both acts are holy in His sight.

~

*Thought*: The primary boundary God has given us to enjoy sex safely is the marriage covenant.

*Readings*: Malachi 2:13–16; 1 Corinthians 6:12–20

# — DAY 70 —
## DIFFERENCES IN COMMUNICATION STYLES

*"We have different gifts, according to the grace given to each of us."* —Romans 12:6

Paul was writing about spiritual gifts in the above verse, but the same idea applies to the different communication styles men and women display. In His purpose and grace, God made males and females very different from each other in the way they think, act, and respond. These differences were designed to be complementary and not divisive.

In upcoming devotionals, we will be discussing the basic natures and tendencies of men and women in communication. Of course, there will always be exceptions, for every person is unique. Yet within the variations, the general tendencies usually hold true.

Adam and Eve originally lived in harmony with God, and so they were able to live in harmony with one another. They knew how to draw on each other's strengths in communication for the betterment of them both. However, when humanity turned away from God's purposes and broke relationship with Him, the lines of communication between males and females were cut or, at least, badly frayed. Thus, the differences that were originally designed for mutual support now often lead to misunderstandings and conflicts in marriage and in other relationships between men and women.

The chances are very good that you have experienced some of these misunderstandings and conflicts firsthand! Handling differences of opinion and avoiding discord are universal problems in relationships. How can you live harmoniously with a spouse whom you love but who processes information and responds in a manner that is different from the way that you do? Again, men and women must be brought into the complementary balance that was God's original purpose for them. This balance will be achieved when we understand the strengths of each communication style and learn to communicate with each other according to the style that the other party can receive and understand.

With this knowledge—and some patience and forgiveness—men and women who are seeking God's redemptive purposes for their lives can communicate effectively and happily with one another. When they are considerate of each other, they have the basis on which they can develop the mutual love and respect that is crucial to lasting relationships.

*Thought*: We need to learn to communicate with each other according to the style that the other party can receive and understand.

*Readings*: Proverbs 18:21; Romans 12:3–8

# "LOGICAL THINKER"
# AND "EMOTIONAL FEELER"

*"How many are your works, LORD! In wisdom you made them all."*　　　　　　　　　　　　　　—Psalm 104:24

Good made the man chiefly as a "logical thinker" and the woman primarily as an "emotional feeler." This does not mean that women do not use logic or that men do not have emotions. They each just have a specific way of looking at the world. When I state that a woman is an emotional feeler, I am referring to the way in which she processes the verbal and nonverbal communication she receives from the world around her. Because the woman is an incubator, she not only receives thoughts and ideas into her being, but also transforms them as she processes them in her emotional, mental, and spiritual wombs. Her communication style reflects this process. When a woman receives information, she assesses it both mentally and emotionally *at the same time*. This is what makes her distinct from the male, who generally uses these functions separately.

God's creation is remarkable. He actually designed the brains of males and females to be different. The neural pathways between the left and right hemispheres of a woman's brain (both the logical and the emotional sides) are intact. This explains what often puzzles many men: women's ability to do multiple tasks at the same time rather than having to focus on just one. The woman's brain allows her to process facts and feelings almost simultaneously. Her emotions are with her all the time she is thinking, and this influences her perspective on the world around her as well as what is communicated to her.

There are fewer nerves connecting the two hemispheres of the male's brain, so the logical and emotional sides are not as closely connected. Because of this, a man basically needs to "shift gears" to move from his dominant logical side to his emotional side. This is why men, in general, think in terms of facts and in a linear fashion. They think like a straight line—the shortest distance between two points—which gives them the ability to see the goal (the vision) and to focus their energies on reaching it in the most straightforward and direct way.

Women, on the other hand, tend to think more like a grid than a straight line. A woman's brain is designed to pick up many details that men don't "see"—things that go beyond the mere facts, such as the personalities, motivations, and feelings of both herself and others. She can perceive, evaluate, and see relationships between things all at the same time, like x, y, and z coordinates on a grid track multiple factors at the same time.

No one person, and no one gender, can look at the world with complete perspective. Therefore, God has designed things so that when the male and the female work together in unity, they can help one another to see a more balanced picture of life. They weren't meant to understand the world and fulfill their dominion mandate in isolation from one another. For this reason, they have built-in ways of seeing the world that are of benefit to each other.

⟡

*Thought*: No one person, and no one gender, can look at the world with complete perspective.

*Readings*: Psalm 139:1–3; Philippians 4:8

# —Day 72—
## VALUING THE OTHER'S CONTRIBUTION

*"Two are better than one, because they have a good return for their labor: if either of them falls down, one can help the other up."* —Ecclesiastes 4:9–10

The distinct differences between men and women are meant to be a help to them—not a hindrance or a source of pain. One way of thinking and communicating is not better than the other way, and the inherent differences between the two are not a result of the fall of humanity. The way men and women are designed is for their good. They just need to exercise patience and understanding and to value the other's contribution.

The female's emotional feeling will balance the male's logical thinking. Many women don't understand how important they are to the men in their lives. The female was created to help the male in that whatever the man lacks, the woman possesses. The reverse is also true. This principle is based on God's purpose.

If men and women are not careful, they will come to conclusions about each other's motivations without knowing what the woman is really thinking or the man is really feeling. This has caused many people to think that their marriages or relationships aren't working. After a while, they say, "Forget this," and they walk away. Later on, they meet somebody else and get married, hoping things will be different this time. However, they encounter the same problems that they did in their previous relationships. They think the problem is with the other person, when the problem is often with the inability of both parties to communicate well. This cycle will continue until they learn to understand and work through the differences between men and women, why each is unique, and how God has made them to complement one another beautifully.

⌐⏤⏤⏤⏝

*Thought*: The next time you are tempted to label a female as "unthinking," stop and appreciate her unique outlook, which brings balance and perspective to your life.

*Readings*: Ecclesiastes 4:9–12; Ephesians 4:3

# —DAY 73—
# A WOMAN'S INSIGHT
# AND DISCERNMENT

*"While Pilate was sitting on the judge's seat, his wife sent him this message: 'Don't have anything to do with that innocent man, for I have suffered a great deal today in a dream because of him.'"* —Matthew 27:19

Awoman's communication gifts include insight and discernment. Men need to be sensitive to the discernment that God gives to their wives and to other women in their lives. There is an interesting example of this truth in the incident when Pilate judged Jesus.

Pilate was carrying out his job, the administration of Roman authority over the Jews. When the chief priests brought Jesus before Pilate and accused Him of being an insurrectionist, Pilate's first inclination was to rule within the law. He saw no basis for their accusations and wanted to release Jesus. In the middle of this dispute, Pilate's wife sent a warning to him: *"Don't have anything to do with that innocent man."* In essence, she was saying, "I have a premonition about this Man. He didn't do anything wrong. Don't touch Him." She was trying to appeal to Pilate's sensibilities, warning him that he should use discretion when making his decision.

Pilate became nervous that things were getting out of hand when the religious leaders assembled an unruly crowd to demand that Jesus be crucified. He ended up being swayed by this pressure and ordering Jesus's death. He may have justified his decision by telling himself that it was logical: keeping order for Rome should take precedence over preserving the life of one innocent man. Even though Pilate knew Jesus had done nothing wrong, he had Him crucified. He would have done better to listen to the instincts of his wife.

⌢

*Thought*: Men need to be sensitive to the discernment that God gives to their wives and to other women for their benefit.

*Readings*: Proverbs 31:10–12, 26; Matthew 27:11–26

# DIFFERENCES IN PROBLEM SOLVING

*"Speaking the truth in love, we will grow to become in every respect the mature body of him who is the head, that is, Christ."* —Ephesians 4:15

Men and women's distinct approaches to problem solving often cause them to react differently to life's difficulties or to conflicts in interpersonal relationships.

Men generally are like filing cabinets: they make decisions quickly and "file" them away in their minds. Or, they put a problem in a mental "to do" folder and go on to other things. They reopen the folder only when they feel ready to deal with it. In contrast, women generally are like computers. Their minds keep working things through until a problem is solved.

Men tend to be resentful about problems, and it's harder for them to see past their anger. They might just "file away" their problems and ignore them for a while. On the other hand, women are guilt-prone; therefore, they often feel responsible for situations, whether they have caused them or not. Even if they are angry, they will look within to see what they could have done differently or how they can resolve the situation.

Men and women can eliminate much frustration in their relationships by understanding each other's problem-solving strengths and using them to benefit one another. For instance, a woman can assist a man in resolving a problem with a coworker by talking through the difficulty with him and helping him to recognize the motivations and feelings involved. A man can help a woman reach a decision more quickly by acknowledging her feelings about a situation but also clearly outlining for her the facts and options involved. Taking into consideration both intuitive and factual information will help men and women to make better decisions.

$\sim$

*Thought*: Distinct approaches to problem solving are often the reason men and women will react differently to life's difficulties or conflicts in interpersonal relationships.

*Readings*: Proverbs 2:6; James 1:5–6

# —Day 75—
## DIFFERENCES IN REALIZING GOALS

*"From* [Christ] *the whole body, joined and held together by every supporting ligament, grows and builds itself up in love, as each part does its work."* —Ephesians 4:16

When it comes to material things, such as a job task, a building project, or financial planning, men want to know the details of how to get there. They like to know what steps they must take to achieve a task. In contrast, women tend to look at overall goals. They think about what they want to accomplish rather than focusing on a step-by-step outline of what needs to be done. While a man will sit down and write out a list of points, a woman might just start doing something to make sure it gets done.

However, when it comes to spiritual or intangible things, the opposite is generally true: males look at overall goals, while females want to know how to get there. These tendencies are why men usually remember the gist of a matter, while women often remember the details and overlook the gist. Men are interested in the principle, the abstract, the philosophy. They see the general direction they need to go in spiritually, and they head toward it. As long as they know what they believe, they don't always see the need for activities designed to help them arrive at their goal. However, women like to be involved in the process. They will attend prayer meetings and Bible studies, read Christian books, and participate more in the life of the church because it will help them grow spiritually.

Men and women can bring balance to one another in both material and spiritual things by helping each other to keep visions and goals clearly in mind while identifying the steps that are necessary to accomplish them effectively.

⌒

*Thought*: When it comes to spiritual things, males look at overall goals, while females want to know how to get there. Men see the general direction they need to go in, while women like to be involved in the process.

*Readings*: Proverbs 3:5–6; Philippians 3:12–14

# DIFFERENCES IN PERSONALITY
# AND SELF-PERCEPTION

*"Love is patient, love is kind. It does not envy, it does not boast, it is not proud. It does not dishonor others, it is not self-seeking, it is not easily angered, it keeps no record of wrongs. Love does not delight in evil but rejoices with the truth. It always protects, always trusts, always hopes, always perseveres."*
—1 Corinthians 13:4–7

Generally, a man's job is an extension of his personality, whereas a woman's home is an extension of hers. This difference can cause much conflict in relationships. A woman may want her husband to spend time with her at home, but he can enjoy working twelve hours a day away from the home because he's cultivating something that is a reflection of who he is. When a man loses his job, it can be devastating to his self-esteem because he considers his job to be almost synonymous with himself.

A woman places high value on her physical surroundings and on creating a home. Men don't understand why women become upset when they track sawdust in the living room after it has just been vacuumed. Men are not trying to be inconsiderate; they just don't think in the same terms that women do. When the beauty and order of the home are disturbed, it can be unsettling for a woman.

Another aspect of the differences in male and female personality is that men's personalities are fairly consistent, while women are continually changing. Women seek personal growth and development more than men do. They like to redecorate the home, discover new skills, or gain a new outlook. Men are often satisfied to follow the same routines, think in the same patterns, and wear the same suits—for twenty years!

Understanding these differences in personality traits is essential because they involve sensitive areas of our lives, such as what we value and how we perceive ourselves. Men and women can use their knowledge of these distinctions to build up each another's self-esteem and to give each other latitude when they view life differently.

⌒

*Thought*: Women often seek personal growth and development while men are often satisfied to follow the same routines.

*Readings*: Genesis 2:8–15; 2 Peter 3:18

# DIFFERENCES IN IDEAS OF SECURITY AND COMFORT

*"God is our refuge and strength, an ever-present help in trouble. Therefore we will not fear, though the earth give way and the mountains fall into the heart of the sea, though its waters roar and foam and the mountains quake with their surging."*
— Psalm 46:1–3

Because men put a strong emphasis on their jobs and are not as emotionally connected to their physical surroundings, they have a tendency to be nomadic as they look for new career opportunities. Conversely, many women have a great need for security and roots. While a move due to a new job seems like an adventure for a man and signals progress in his career, it can be stressful and difficult for his wife, who may have to leave family and friends behind for an uncertain future. Women will also change geographic locations for jobs; however, married women are less willing to make a move to advance their own jobs than they are for their husbands' jobs. They are less inclined to want to disrupt the lives of their families, especially when they have children.

On the other hand, when it comes to encountering something new, men tend to stand back and evaluate at first. Women are more ready to accept new experiences, and they participate in them more easily.

Matters involving security and comfort can require great understanding on the part of a spouse. They reflect issues such as fulfillment, trustworthiness, fear, and feelings of instability. When men or women want to make job changes or embark on something new, they should be aware of the possible reactions of their spouses and show kindness and patience as they work through these potential changes to their lives.

<hr/>

*Thought*: Matters involving security and comfort can require great understanding on the part of a spouse because they reflect issues such as fulfillment, trustworthiness, fear, and feelings of instability.

*Readings*: Psalm 46; Romans 15:13

# — DAY 78 —
# ARE YOU MOVING TOWARD GOD OR AWAY FROM HIM?

*"See, I lay a stone in Zion, a chosen and precious cornerstone,*
*and the one who trusts in him will never be put to shame."*
—1 Peter 2:6

When humanity rejected God, He gave them what they wanted. He gave them over to their passions. That's not as simple as it might sound. If God had just given us over to what we wanted, the implication might have been that we could succeed in spite of Him. But when God gave us over, He also allowed us to experience the inevitable results of our actions. He didn't just say, "Okay, go, carry on." He said, "If you carry on, you're going to end up depraved, because that isn't the way I made you." (See Romans 1:28.)

The principle here is that you cannot move away from God and be successful. You cannot cut off your relationship with the Manufacturer and expect to find genuine parts somewhere else. Any part you find on your own will not function properly.

God says that when we reject His purposes, He gives us over to a depraved mind. In other words, He tells us, "Without Me, your mind isn't going to get any better; it will only get worse." Therefore, if we think we can find out how to be better men or women without God, we are in trouble, for the consequences are serious. When we believe that we don't need God, we get worse and worse. If you don't want to live in God's purpose for humanity, then you will end up doing yourself harm.

People all over the world are creating businesses and industries, amassing wealth, constructing houses, making ships and aircraft, and pursuing similar endeavors. They are building, building, building, but their lives are falling apart—their spouses are leaving them, their kids are on drugs, and they don't have any sense of what is really important in life. They have much wealth, but everything is coming apart because they lack a vital relationship with God, and they're missing the Chief Cornerstone. Some of you reading this devotional would admit that you haven't wanted Jesus Christ in your life. Yet you need Him! He is essential to your life. He is not optional.

Today, when we dedicate a school, a church, or another building, we often put a plaque on the bottom corner of the building. That's not a real cornerstone but a ceremonial one that is based on the real, functional cornerstones of the past. Whose name goes on a cornerstone? It could be the owner of the building or perhaps the contractor. If you go to Greece and Rome today, you can still see who built many of the ancient buildings because their names are carved in the cornerstones.

Whose name is on your cornerstone? If it's anything besides Jesus Christ, I can tell you the future of your building. It will ultimately fall. But the Scripture assures us, *"The one who trusts in him [Jesus] will never be put to shame"* (1 Peter 2:6).

⌒

*Thought*: Jesus Christ is not optional—He is vital to your life.

*Readings*: Isaiah 9:6–7; John 14:1–14

# — DAY 79 —
## PRAYER IS ESSENTIAL FOR GOD'S WILL

*"For Yours is the kingdom and the power and the glory forever."* —Matthew 6:13 (NKJV)

As human beings, our need to pray results from the way God arranged dominion on the earth. God made the world. Then He made men and women, giving them dominion over the works of His hands. When God said, *"Let them rule...over all the earth"* (Genesis 1:26 NIV84), He ordered the dominion of the world in a way that made rule by humans essential to accomplishing His purposes. He causes things to happen on earth when men and women are in agreement with His will. Prayer, therefore, is essential for God's will to be done in the earth. Since God never breaks His Word concerning how things are to work, prayer is mandatory, not optional, for spiritual progress.

God's plan is for mankind to desire what He desires, to will what He wills, and to ask Him to accomplish His purposes in the world so that goodness and truth, rather than evil and darkness, may reign on the earth. In this sense, by praying, we give God the freedom to intervene in earth's affairs.

Even before God's plan of redemption was fully accomplished in Christ, God used humans to fulfill His will. We see this truth in the lives of Abraham, Moses, Gideon, David, Daniel, and many others. God continued to work with mankind to fulfill His purposes on earth even though man's part was limited by his sin and lack of understanding of God's ways.

As a man created in the image of God, dominion authority is your heritage. God desires that you will His will. His will should be the foundation of your prayers, the heart of your intercession, and the source of your confidence in supplication.

When we know and obey God's will, and ask Him to fulfill it, He will grant our request. Whether we are praying for individual, family, community, national, or world needs, we must seek to be in agreement with God's will so His purposes can reign on the earth. This is the essence of exercising dominion.

*Thought*: God causes things to happen on earth when men and women are in agreement with His will.

*Readings*: Isaiah 55:10–11; Matthew 6:5–14

# YOUR HEAVENLY COMPASS

*"If any of you lacks wisdom, you should ask God, who gives generously to all without finding fault, and it will be given to you. But when you ask, you must believe and not doubt, because the one who doubts is like a wave of the sea, blown and tossed by the wind. That person should not expect to receive anything from the Lord. Such a person is double-minded and unstable in all they do."* —James 1:5–8

Remember that you are the anchor of your family's "boat," keeping it steady in storms as you hold securely to Jesus, your Rock. Yet Jesus also has given us a Compass, the Holy Spirit, to give us our bearings and direction in life. He will teach and strengthen you; He will guide your conscience and establish your convictions so you can reach shore safely. James wrote that God will give wisdom generously to everyone *"without finding fault."* Yet we need to exercise faith when we ask, or we will be *"blown and tossed by the wind."* Our anchor will not be secure but *"unstable."*

The word *Bahamas* means "shallow waters," but there's a place where the sea drops off about six thousand feet, which is called the tongue of the ocean. Once, my associates and I had gone spear fishing, and we were diving at a reef right next to the tongue. As long as our boat stayed in the shallow area, the anchor held because it could reach rock at the bottom. But then the anchor got into some sand, and the current from the tongue of the ocean started dragging the boat.

When the boat drifted over the tongue, the anchor had nothing to hold on to; it was thousands of feet above the bottom of the ocean. When we noticed what was happening, we were on the reef yelling for the captain to come, and he was trying to start the engine, but the engine wouldn't start! He was drifting over the depths of the ocean.

That was a moment I'll never forget. We were about fifty feet from the tongue where there were massive sharks. We were stranded on the reef, there was a strong current that could pull us toward the tongue, and our only refuge was that boat. At that point, the boat's anchor was useless as our security because it had nothing to hold on to. After being out all night in the darkness, we were finally rescued. Our families had contacted the equivalent of the Coast Guard in the Bahamas, and a ship came and found us. Similarly, you can call on the Holy Spirit's help. He will direct and protect you in both the calm and stormy seas of your life. Even if there is darkness all around you, He will guide you in the right direction.

*Thought*: The Holy Spirit will direct and protect you in both the calm and stormy seas of your life.

*Readings*: Psalm 139:1–12; Romans 8:26–28

# TOO TOUGH TO WORSHIP?

*"Great is the* Lord, *and greatly to be praised; and His greatness is unsearchable."* —Psalm 145:3 (nkjv)

Some men have been restored to their heavenly Father through Christ, but they have the idea that they're too tough to worship Him, as if it isn't manly. Let me ask you: who wrote much of the book in the Bible that's filled with worship and praise? It was a man who killed a lion and a bear with his bare hands. He killed a ten-foot giant with a rock.

Anyone can sit down in a pew and fold his arms. It takes a giant-slayer like David to write things like, *"O* Lord, *our Lord, how majestic is your name in all the earth! You have set your glory above the heavens"* (Psalm 8:1 niv84), and *"I will extol the* Lord *at all times; his praise will always be on my lips. My soul will boast in the* Lord*"* (Psalm 34:1–2 niv84). I love to worship more than anything else. I've led worship in our church for years. I've written books on it. Worship is the most important thing in my life because it protects the rest of my life and gives glory to God.

Psalm 150:6 says, *"Let everything that has breath praise the* Lord*."* Yet, when many men go to church, they feel ashamed to lift their hands to the God who made them. Satan doesn't want you ever to feel comfortable worshipping God, because when you worship Him, you attract His presence. When you become ashamed of public worship, you are an embarrassment to God's assignment for you as a man. On Sunday, you should be the first one at church, sitting up front, because you are the worship leader of your family—not your wife, sisters, or daughters. Remember, the first thing that makes you a man is your capacity to enter Eden—the presence of your God.

*Thought*: Worship is the most important thing in my life because it protects the rest of my life and gives glory to God.

*Readings*: Psalm 150; Ephesians 5:18–20

# THE IMPORTANCE OF FORGIVENESS

*"Therefore, if you are offering your gift at the altar and there remember that your brother or sister has something against you, leave your gift there in front of the altar. First go and be reconciled to them; then come and offer your gift."*
—Matthew 5:23–24

J esus talked a great deal about the importance of forgiveness in our relationships. He said that if you do not forgive someone who has something against you, or whom you have something against, then the Father will not forgive you and will not hear you. Jesus was saying that relationships with other people are even more important than worship, because you cannot worship except in the context of your relationships.

It doesn't matter how serious and sincere you are about God. It doesn't matter how filled you are with the Holy Spirit or how much Scripture you've learned. God is not overly impressed by your ability to communicate with Him, by your ability to articulate your worship, prayer, or praise. His reception of your worship—whether it is through your giving, your praise, your administration of the kingdom of God, or your ministry of the gifts of the Spirit—is contingent upon your relationships with others, especially your spouse. So, if you give God a thousand dollars, whether or not God receives it depends on whether or not you are in right relationship with others. God's acceptance of even your tithes is contingent upon your relationships with other people, not on how much you give Him.

Thus, a right relationship with God is dependent on right relationships with other people. This truth brings the matter of reconciled relationships between men and women down to where it hurts, doesn't it? We must understand clearly what God's Word says so that we have no excuse for failing to mend our broken relationships.

Can you imagine husbands and wives stopping in the middle of Sunday morning worship and stepping outside to make things right with each other? If that were to happen, we'd have a brand-new church and society. Yet I find that people often try the easy route when they have been in conflict with others. They go to God and say, "God, please forgive Mary," "God, tell Mary that I forgive her," or "God, I ask You to change Mary." They don't want to go to the person directly. We love to hide behind God so we don't have to accept the responsibility of face-to-face relationships. Our reluctance to deal honestly and directly with others is the reason why there are so many problems in relationships, even in the body of Christ.

I honor my wife and do right by her, not only because I love her, but also for the sake of my relationship with God. *"Husbands,... be considerate as you live with your wives...so that nothing will hinder your prayers"* (1 Peter 3:7). Jesus said that my relationship with God is even more important than my relationship with my wife— and yet God made my relationship with Him contingent on my relationship with her.

*Thought*: You cannot worship God except in the context of your relationships.

*Readings*: Genesis 50:15–21; Mark 11:24–25

# DON'T BECOME CRACKED
# OR SIDETRACKED

*"In him [Jesus] the whole building is joined together and rises to become a holy temple in the Lord."* —Ephesians 2:21

W e have seen that the key to constructing any building is the structure's foundation, because the foundation carries the weight of the building. The quality of a foundation determines the stability and value of what is built upon it. Having the characteristics of a strong foundation is therefore essential for every man.

A building can have a number of problems and not be condemned. But if a crack is discovered in the foundation, it doesn't matter how nice the interior is, the building will need serious repair and may well be condemned. Men, we need to be careful not to allow any cracks in our character. If you see a crack developing, fix it immediately! Do not let it get any bigger, or the whole structure may collapse. You may think that character lapses affect only you, but they also affect those entrusted to your protection, teaching, and care. Strengthen your character, and you will strengthen your entire family.

*Make every effort to add to your faith goodness; and to goodness, knowledge; and to knowledge, self-control; and to self-control, perseverance; and to perseverance, godliness; and to godliness, brotherly kindness; and to brotherly kindness, love. For if you possess these qualities in increasing measure, they will keep you from being ineffective and unproductive in your knowledge of our Lord Jesus Christ.*

(2 Peter 1:5–8 NIV84)

We have also seen that discovering our purpose enables us to stop wasting our lives and start fulfilling our potential. So we must be careful not to become sidetracked along the way. The greatest way to destroy someone is to distract the person from his or her true purpose.

Remember that, in the Old Testament, Nehemiah fulfilled an important purpose in life, but he might have become sidetracked. He was in exile serving as cupbearer to the king of Persia when he heard that Jerusalem was still in a broken-down condition. He was distressed and determined, "I've got to repair the city." So he prayed, and he obtained permission from the king to rebuild the wall of Jerusalem. God's favor was on his plans because this was the purpose for which he had been created. He went and started to rebuild the wall with the help of the remnant of Jews in Jerusalem.

Some men near Jerusalem didn't like what Nehemiah was doing, and they tried to stop him. They ridiculed and slandered him, but he kept on with the work. They conspired to kill him, but he armed some of the workers and thwarted the plot. They tried to fill him with fear and make him flee for his life, but he remained steadfast. One of the last things they tried is usually the most effective means of sidetracking people. They said, "Come, let's have a meeting; let's discuss what you're doing. Maybe we can help you." (See Nehemiah 1–6.) Yet Nehemiah wasn't fooled. He told them, "*I am carrying on a great project and cannot go down. Why should the work stop while I leave it and go down to you?*" (Nehemiah 6:3).

Likewise, don't be distracted from your purpose in God!

*Thought*: If you see a crack developing, fix it immediately!

*Readings*: Psalm 1:1–3; Galatians 5:7–8

# —Day 84—
## PREPARED FOR THE STORM

*"The eternal God is your refuge, and underneath are the everlasting arms."*  —Deuteronomy 33:27

To everything there is a season, a time for every purpose under heaven" (Ecclesiastes 3:1 NKJV). Everything in life has a season. This means that whatever difficulties we're experiencing are not going to last. However, it also means that whatever we are enjoying now may not last, either. Many of us do not want to hear this; we think that everything is forever.

Let me remind you that even if you are in Christ Jesus, you are not immune to life's storms. When we look at people who are men and women of God, who are faithful in service to Him, who are praying people, or who have served others greatly, but who still find themselves in crises, we say, "This isn't supposed to happen to people like them." As Jesus indicated in one of His parables, it doesn't matter what kind of "house" you have—whether built on sand or rock—the storm is coming. The issue is not really the storm. The issue is the foundation. Remember that as you hold on to the Rock, your foundation will remain sure. (See Matthew 7:24–27.)

I've lived in the Bahamas all my life, and God has used the ocean to teach me essential lessons on Christian living. Often, my friends and I have gone out on our boats early in the morning to fish, and the water is like glass as we speed over the ocean. By one o'clock in the afternoon, however, a storm may be coming, and, since we're ten miles from shore, we have to start tying everything down. The season has changed, and the boat will rock during the storm, but everyone knows what to do. We've already been trained; we've prepared for the storm.

We know to put the anchor down. We actually dive down and put that anchor under the rock. Then, we brace everything. When the storm is upon us, it's too late to do anything else; the season has come. We're beaten about by the wind and waves, but after about fifteen or twenty minutes, it passes us by. Then, it's peaceful again, and we can go back to fishing.

It will be the same with you. Once you have committed to the Rock and have prepared for the changing seasons of life, you will be able to ride out the storm and then go back to fishing. It's going to be all right, and it's going to be even better fishing because the storm will have stirred up more fish. Behind every broken experience is a wealthy experience from the Lord. There is peace in the promise that nothing earthly lasts, but the Rock is eternal.

⌒

*Thought*: You are not immune to storms. Are you holding on to the Rock?

*Readings*: Psalm 62:5–8; Matthew 7:24–27

# —DAY 85—
## A TEMPTATION OR A TEST?

*"God cannot be tempted by evil, nor does he tempt anyone."*
—James 1:13

The Bible assures us that God doesn't tempt us. He may test us, however. (See, for example, 2 Chronicles 32:31.) What's the difference between a test and a temptation? A test is more like the act of tempering metal.

The Greeks and Romans used tempering in the process of making swords for battle. They would put a piece of steel in the fire until it became so hot you could see into it and determine if there were any black spots in it. The black spots were areas in which the molecules were not close enough together; they were weak areas. When they discovered any spots, they would put the hot sword on a steel anvil and pound it with a steel mallet. As they struck the spots, the molecules would come together. They would keep pounding until they couldn't see any more spots.

Next, they would put the sword in cold water, and the steel would harden. After that, they would put the sword back in the fire until it became hot and malleable again. They would continue this cycle—fire, beating, cold water—until they couldn't see any more spots.

After a sword had gone through this process, they could be sure it would not break in the middle of a battle where a soldier's life depended on it. You never trust a sword that has not been tempered.

This process is similar to how God tests us. *Tempering means testing for weakness to insure strength.* God doesn't need the tempering process in order to see your true character. He can already see into you, and He knows your secret "spots." He knows your habits, your weaknesses, the garbage you have hidden away. The tempering is for your sake. He allows you to go through trials and tests so you can recognize what is hindering your life.

⌒

*Thought*: Tempering means testing for weakness to insure strength.

*Readings*: Psalm 66:10; 1 Peter 1:6–7

# —DAY 86—
## THE ANCHOR MUST HOLD

*"Now no chastening seems to be joyful for the present, but painful; nevertheless, afterward it yields the peaceable fruit of righteousness to those who have been trained by it."*
—Hebrews 12:11 (NKJV)

Anchors are designed to secure a ship; that's why they must be tested. It's too late to test them in an emergency. When a ship is heading toward a rocky shore, its anchor must hold. Similarly, when men's families run into problems, *they* must hold. They have to hold those families together.

If you are a male living at home with your mother and sisters, and your father is absent, you are the "father" of that house. Your mother wasn't designed to fill that purpose. Jesus took over His family's leadership after Joseph died. And He made sure with His last breaths that His mother would be secured in John's household after He was gone. He said to His mother, *"'Dear woman, here is your son,' and to the disciple, 'Here is your mother'"* (John 19:26–27 NIV84). He was being the sustainer of His mother.

When the anchor of a family fails, disaster is inevitable. If you walk out on your marriage, you will not only destroy your family, but you will also damage the community. If you're a pastor and things aren't going right and you abandon the pulpit before God calls you to leave, you will cause problems in the body of Christ. That's not a personal decision anymore because you're called to be the anchor.

Remember that storms are only for a season. You are being tested to insure your strength. You will come back from the storms better than ever, in a way others have never seen you before. Your best years are still ahead of you. Let God refine you, and a new man will emerge. You are an anchor. Protect your ship throughout the journey so that it can arrive at its destination safely.

*Thought*: Let God refine you, and a new man will emerge.

*Readings*: Proverbs 17:3; Hebrews 12:1–13

## — DAY 87 —
# REFLECTING GOD'S NATURE
# TO THE WORLD

*"There are also celestial bodies and terrestrial bodies; but the glory of the celestial is one, and the glory of the terrestrial is another. There is one glory of the sun, another glory of the moon, and another glory of the stars; for one star differs from another star in glory."* —1 Corinthians 15:40–41 (NKJV)

When we think of *"glory,"* we often think of a cloud filled with light. Yet glory in the sense of the above passage has to do with the nature of something. In its larger meaning, the word *glory* can be ascribed to every single thing. *The glory of something is its best expression of itself.*

One of the definitions of *glory* is "a distinguished quality or asset." You can see a flower in its true glory when it is in full bloom. You can see a leopard or a lion in its true glory when it is at its prime strength. You can see the sun in its true glory at twelve noon; after that, its light begins to fade. The glory of a thing is when it is at its full, true self. Therefore, glory refers to the manifestation, or the exposure, of the true nature of something.

When the Bible says that the purpose of humanity is to manifest the glory of God, it does not mean just lifting one's hands and saying, "Hallelujah!" That is praise, but it is not glory in the sense in which we are speaking. *Reflecting the glory of God means reflecting His true nature.* God's glory is often best manifested when we respond in a Christlike way in a difficult situation. At that moment, God is saying to you, "Let the glory come out now. Let people see what God is like under pressure."

*Thought:* God's glory is often best manifested when we respond in a Christlike way in a difficult situation.

*Readings:* Isaiah 60:1–3; Philippians 2:14–16

# 10 KEYS TO TRUE MANHOOD, PART 1

*"You have made known to me the path of life; you will fill me with joy in your presence, with eternal pleasures at your right hand."* —Psalm 16:11 (NIV84)

You must realize that you are *born* a male, but you have to *become* a man. This means that someone could actually grow up to be just an old male, never living as a real man. We have learned that a male can be transformed into the man God purposed when He created the world. Becoming God's man is the only way a male can live a satisfying and meaningful life, because His purpose is the key to fulfillment.

A man is responsible for living out God's purposes in the world and enabling others to do so, also. In the final three days of this devotional, meditate on the following keys—all of which come down to a stewardship of the lives and resources with which God has entrusted us—until the true meaning of what it is to be a man permeates your understanding, and His presence and purpose overflow from your life to the world around you.

*Key #1: A real man desires and loves God.* A real man seeks intimate communion with God by remaining continually in His presence. He loves to worship the One who created and redeemed him. *"You will fill me with joy in your presence."* A real man is clear about what his priorities are.

*Key #2: A real man seeks to restore God's image in himself.* A real man wants to be spiritually renewed so that the fullness of God's image and likeness is restored to his life. He seeks to return to the original plan that God intended when He first made human beings. A real man is not deceived by or enamored of counterfeit images of manhood, such as the popular culture presents. He wants to be what he was created to be. He wants to be like his Father God.

*Key #3: A real man aspires to work and to develop his gifts and talents.* A real man's motivation for work is to fulfill the purposes for which he was created. He aspires to do the work of God the Father while developing and using the gifts and talents God has given him. He isn't lazy; he has a vision for his life, and he is willing to work to fulfill it. In the garden of Eden, there was no supervisor, no one to hand out paychecks. Work was given to Adam because it was a natural part of his being. Through work, he fulfilled his purpose as a man. God wants us to go to work to multiply His kingdom on earth.

*Key #4: A real man honors his marriage and family above personal interests.* Jesus loves His betrothed, the bride of Christ. He is a family Man, and He takes care of her. The Bible says that He gave His life for the church. He cleanses her *"by the washing with water through the word"* (Ephesians 5:26). A man is to love his wife *"just as Christ loved the church and gave himself up for her.... Husbands ought to love their wives as their own bodies"* (verses 25, 28). A real man protects and takes care of his wife and family, looking out for their needs before his own. A few real men who truly understood this truth and endeavored to live it out could set a standard for entire nations.

*Thought*: You are born a male, but you have to become a man.

*Readings*: Isaiah 6:8; John 4:34

# 10 KEYS TO TRUE MANHOOD, PART 2

*"I have hidden your word in my heart that I might not sin against you.… I meditate on your precepts and consider your ways. I delight in your decrees; I will not neglect your word."*
—Psalm 119:11, 15–16

*Key #5: A real man endeavors to learn, live, and teach God's Word and principles.* In Genesis 2:15–17, God commanded the first man to keep His word, saying that if he disobeyed it, he would die. In this act, He established the principle that *"man does not live on bread alone, but on every word that comes from the mouth of God"* (Matthew 4:4 niv84). A real man is a man of principles. He realizes that his spirit must be nourished by the Word of God or his spiritual health will decline. God's Word determines the precepts by which he lives. Because he is a responsible leader, he is also committed to teaching the Scriptures to his family. A real man allows the Word to transform his life so that he can represent God's will on earth, thus spreading the garden of God's presence to a world living in the darkness of sin and separation from God.

*Key #6: A real man demonstrates faith and inspires it in others.* Jesus said, *"Nothing is impossible with God"* (Luke 1:37 niv84). When you return to God's original image for men, you become a person who helps people believe that anything is possible. A real man has a spirit of faith and inspires others. Counterfeit men have no faith. But, even in the darkest hour, a real man believes there's a way out. He will tell you a thousand times, "Get up again; you can do it." A real man might be scared, but he won't worry, because he trusts in God to finish the work He began. The faith of a real man believes in what God said, not in what he sees.

*Key #7: A real man is committed to cultivating others to be the best they can be.* A real man encourages others to reflect the image and creativity of God in all they are and do—spiritually, emotionally, psychologically, and physically. He prays for wisdom and guidance on how to cultivate his wife and children so they can mature in Christ and become all that God has created them to be. He encourages his family to develop their gifts and talents in any way he can. He delights in seeing these gifts unfold in their lives, just as God delights in seeing us use our abilities for His glory.

*Thought*: A real man allows the Word to transform his life so that he can represent God's will on earth.

*Readings*: Psalm 119:1–18; Romans 12:1–2

# 10 KEYS TO TRUE MANHOOD, PART 3

*"He has shown you, O mortal, what is good. And what does the LORD require of you? To act justly and to love mercy and to walk humbly with your God."* —Micah 6:8

*Key #8: A real man loves compassion, mercy, and justice.* By exercising compassion, mercy, and justice, he shows true strength and brings the kingdom of God to others. *Compassion* is passion that is aimed at setting people free. To show compassion means to apply one's strength to meet people's needs. *Mercy* is not treating people as they deserve when they have committed wrongs against you. We are not to seek revenge against others, but to freely forgive them and do everything we can to lead them to Christ. *Justice* means doing what is right by others. God hates injustice. A real man reflects His nature and character by following His command to *"act justly and to love mercy and to walk humbly with your God"* (Micah 6:8).

*Key #9: A real man is faithful to the kingdom of God and His church.* In Matthew 6:33, Jesus reduced life to one thing: *"Seek first his kingdom and his righteousness, and all these things will be given to you as well."* A real man has a passion to see the kingdom of God established. Jesus was excited about men setting other men free. (See, for example, Luke 10:1–21.) Real men have the spirit of the Great Commission in their lives: a love for souls and a passion for others to know Christ.

*Key #10: A real man keeps himself in God.* Our final key is that a real man doesn't take God's presence in his life for granted. He guards his heart and actions so that he can stay close to God and continually reflect His character and ways. He puts the entire weight of his trust in the Lord because he knows that God is *"able to keep* [him] *from falling and to present* [him] *before his glorious presence without fault and with great joy"* (Jude 1:24 NIV84).

Communities and nations will be transformed when men return to God and His purposes for them. God is looking for those who will dedicate themselves to standing *"in the gap on behalf of the land"* (Ezekiel 22:30). He wants to bring His life-changing power to broken marriages, damaged families, shattered societies, and individual men, women, and children who need reconciliation with God and a restoration of His purposes for them. But He's waiting for men like you. Real men who will commit themselves to fulfilling their dominion purpose of spreading God's presence throughout the whole world. I pray that people will be able to look at your life and say, "Now I know what a real man looks like," as they are transformed by God's presence in you.

⌒

*Thought*: A real man has a passion to see the kingdom of God established.

*Readings*: Isaiah 61:1–4; Matthew 28:18–20

# ABOUT THE AUTHOR

Dr. Myles Munroe (1954–2014) was an international motivational speaker, best-selling author, educator, leadership mentor, and consultant for government and business. Traveling extensively throughout the world, Dr. Munroe addressed critical issues affecting the full range of human, social, and spiritual development. He was a popular author of more than forty books, including *The Power of Character in Leadership, The Purpose and Power of Authority, The Principles and Benefits of Change, Becoming a Leader, The Purpose and Power of the Holy Spirit, The Spirit of Leadership, The Principles and Power of Vision, Understanding the Purpose and Power of Prayer, Understanding the Purpose and Power of Women,* and *Understanding the Purpose and Power of Men.* Dr. Munroe was founder and president of Bahamas Faith Ministries International (BFMI), a multidimensional organization headquartered in Nassau, Bahamas. He was chief executive officer and chairman of the board of the International Third World Leaders Association, president of the International Leadership Training Institute, and the founder and executive producer of a number of radio and television programs aired worldwide.

Dr. Munroe earned B.A. and M.A. degrees from Oral Roberts University and the University of Tulsa, and was awarded a number of honorary doctoral degrees. He also served as an adjunct professor of the Graduate School of Theology at Oral Roberts University.

The parents of two adult children, Charisa and Chairo (Myles Jr.), Dr. Munroe and his wife, Ruth, traveled as a team and were involved in teaching seminars together. Both were leaders who ministered with sensitive hearts and international vision. In November 2014, they were tragically killed in an airplane crash en route to an annual leadership conference sponsored by Bahamas Faith Ministries International. A statement from Dr. Munroe in his book *The Power of Character in Leadership* summarizes his own legacy: "Remember that character ensures the longevity of leadership, and men and women of principle will leave important legacies and be remembered by future generations."